CONTENTS

Page

SECTION 1   BASIC DOCTRINES

5   Session 1   WILL THE REAL JESUS PLEASE STAND UP?   Selected passages
                (Understanding Jesus)
                What is Jesus really like?
10   Session 2   THE DECEIVER (Defeating Satan)   Selected passages
                Who is the devil and how can he be defeated?
16   Session 3   ALL OF ME (God and the "whole" person)   Selected passages
                Have I given my *whole* life to Christ?
21   Session 4   GOD'S FOREVER FAMILY (Commitment to the Church)   Selected passages
                How important is the church?

SECTION 2   CHRISTIAN GROWTH

26   Session 5   I AM SOMEBODY (True identity)   Psalm 139/Selected passages
                Who am I?
32   Session 6   THE POSSIBLE DREAM (Hope in Christ)   Romans 8
                Who can I turn to in my despair?
36   Session 7   WHAT'S THE DIFFERENCE? (Confidence in the Christian life)   Selected passages
                What difference does Christ make in daily life?
40   Session 8   GOD! AND HOW? (Making Christ Lord)   Romans 6:11-19
                How can I put God at the center of my life?

SECTION 3   CHRISTIAN LIVING

47   Session 9   MINORITY TACTICS (Taking the offensive in witnessing)   Philippians 1:12-30; 2:1-18
                How can I share my faith with my friends?
51   Session 10   NOT GUILTY! (Finding forgiveness in Christ)   1 John 1:7–2:2
                What can I do about my guilt feelings?
56   Session 11   A MATTER OF LIFE AND DEATH (Understanding death)   James 4:13-15; Philippians 1:20-26
                What's the purpose for my life?
61   Session 12   THAT'S A NO-NO! (Building Christian convictions)   Selected passages
                How do I know how God wants me to act?

SECTION 4   RELATIONSHIPS

66   Session 13   JUST FRIENDS (Building solid friendships)   Selected passages
                How can I be a true friend?
71   Session 14   DATES TO REMEMBER (Understanding "Christian" dating)   Selected passages
                How should a Christian act on a date?
76   Session 15   BROTHERS AND SISTERS (Getting along with siblings)   1 John 2:9-11; 4:19-21
                How can I get along better with my brothers and sisters?   1 Timothy 5:8

HOW TO USE AN *ANY OLD TIME*

SonPower *Any Old Times* (AOTs) are designed to meet a need expressed by many youth leaders—to have a series of topical, self-contained meeting ideas in a format that will "plug in" to their existing programs. Each AOT session is biblical, easy to use, and requires minimal preparation. This book of *Any Old Times* is geared to high school teens, but every session has suggestions for adapting the material to a junior high level.

Each basic session is compact (about 30 minutes) so it can be used "any old time"—after a hayride, on a retreat, during your regular youth group meeting, or just about anywhere. But all sessions can be expanded by using the optional activities included—games, suggestions for further study, additional resources, and so forth. (Optional activities are shaded throughout this book.)

Every AOT session contains three sections: an exercise or activity to arouse the teens' interest in the topic (*Warm-up*), a biblical examination of the subject with discussion questions and/or other activities (*Workout*), and a time for student response (*Wrap-up*). The first page of each session highlights the session goal and provides other necessary information you will need to get started.

(Every session in this book of AOTs has already been proven effective by leaders of Youth for Christ clubs across the United States. We hope the interaction, fun, and potential for spiritual growth within these AOTs will have positive results in *your* group as well.)

SPECIAL FEATURES

Summary page

The first page of each session will show you at a glance the key concept of the session, the goal, a short overview, the estimated time required, any materials or preparations needed, and tips for adapting the session to a junior high age-group.

Topical format

If you want to highlight a particular topic of study, AOTs provide a variety of creative, ready-to-use ideas.

Tips for leaders

The outside columns of the AOT sessions contain helpful hints as you lead the session. You should also find enough room for notes of your own.

Boldface type

The material printed in boldface can be read aloud. Of course, you don't need to read word for word. You should adapt these sections to fit your own unique style of teaching. But the bold type will help guide you through the sections where you will be speaking.

Shaded activities

Any parts of a session that are shaded are optional. These sections can be integrated into the session or skipped, depending on the amount of time you have. You know your specific group better than anyone else, so use your own discretion in using these optional activities.

Adaptability

This is probably the biggest benefit of *Any Old Times*. Each session can be easily adapted to fit your specific time frame, age-group, and meeting format. AOTs can be as flexible as you want them to be.

SESSION 1

WILL THE REAL JESUS PLEASE STAND UP?

WHAT IS JESUS REALLY LIKE?

KEY CONCEPT	Most people have a poor understanding of who Jesus really is, thinking He was just a man who lived 2,000 years ago.
GOAL	This session will help young people realize that Jesus was and is the God-Man, focusing on His claims to be God and the witness of His contemporaries.
OVERVIEW	Though Christian young people believe in the divinity of Christ, many are not sure why. This is, they have never thought it through or checked out the evidence in Scripture. Then, when challenged by friends and others who do *not* believe in Jesus, they don't know what to say. This session is designed, therefore, to build a solid and true understanding of Jesus as the God-Man. Of course, it is not enough to believe the facts about Jesus; we must also live out the implications of our beliefs. Therefore, another emphasis of this session will be to discover what the divinity of Christ should mean in our lives. Also, this session will provide an opportunity to present the plan of salvation if there are non-Christians present.
TIME REQUIRED	30-45 minutes
MATERIALS CHECKLIST	Materials needed for basic session: ____ *Jesus* worksheets ____ Pencils or pens ____ New Testaments ____ Pictures *(Jesus Is. . .)* ____ Chalkboard and chalk or poster board and marker ____ Cards *(Card Challenge)* Materials needed for optional activities: ____ Questionnaires *(Shopping Center Survey)* ____ Magazines and cellophane tape *(Super Superhero)*
JUNIOR HIGH ADAPTATION	When you break into the two groups in the *Workout* section, be sure to have an adult leader for each group. Also, in the groups, keep the discussion concise so that you don't lose their attention. Do *not* use the *Shopping Center Survey* with junior highers.

WARM-UP

Optional Openers

Shopping Center Survey (10 minutes)

If your meeting is close to a shopping center, send your group to the center for a quick survey of ideas about Jesus. Give each person a blank piece of paper and a pencil and the instruction to ask as many people as possible the question, "In a few words, who do you think Jesus was or is?" Make sure they do this about five minutes and then return to the meeting place. When everyone returns, compile the results on the chalkboard or a piece of poster board. If it is not feasible for the whole group to take the survey, a few days before the meeting, take a small delegation and do the survey yourself.

Super Superhero (8 minutes)

Bring a stack of old magazines and distribute them among the group. Also make available a few rolls of cellophane tape. Instruct students to tear out pictures and tape together a "Super Superhero." In other words, they could have a head from one picture, arms from another, clothes from another, etc. They should give their characters names and be ready to explain and describe them to the group. Allow five minutes for the tearing and taping, and then have them display their creations. Take a minute or so to discuss the kinds of heroes we have in society today.

Jesus Is. . . (4 minutes)

Bring a number of pictures or "symbols" of Jesus at various stages of His life on earth. These could include "Baby in the manger," talking with the temple leaders, "Solman's head of Christ," throwing out the money changers from the temple, on the cross, stained-glass picture, etc. Display them one at a time and after each one ask: **If this were all you knew about Jesus, what would be your concept of Him?** Compile a list of their answers.

Discussion (5 minutes)

Ask: **What concepts do people have about Jesus? Who do they think He is or was? What do they think He is or was like?** (Meek and mild; good example to follow; great moral Teacher; counselor; 100-percent God, not man; 100-percent man, not God; etc.) **Where do people get their ideas about Jesus?** (From church, TV preachers, other people, etc.) **In what ways do people "use" Jesus for their own purposes?** (Some invoke His name to support their personal causes; others discount Him and His teaching so they won't feel accountable to Him.) **How can we find out what Jesus is really like?** (Check out the Bible.)

Say something like: **The problem is that everyone wants to put Jesus in a category or slot. If a person can see that Jesus supports his "cause," then he feels better about what he is doing. On the other hand, many people put Jesus into a specific "box" so they don't have to consider Him. But Jesus doesn't fit into our neat little categories. Thus for many He is a real threat to their thinking and ways of life. For a few minutes we are going to examine the primary historical sources to see what Jesus Christ was really like. The eyewitness accounts of Jesus' life are included in Matthew, Mark, Luke, and John.**

Control is very important in this activity. Make sure you instruct the group to be serious and polite at the shopping center, and insist on their return at a specified time. Send your leaders with the group to help.

During the discussion, show how Jesus contrasts with these "Super Heroes" whose main characteristics will revolve around strength and powers.

Sources for these symbols would be Sunday School materials, a nativity scene, various editions of the Bible, "Christian" jewelry, etc.

If you used the *Shopping Center Survey* or another survey, this is the time to make specific references and comparisons with it. Don't get bogged down in this discussion. Its purpose is to set the stage for the Bible study.

WORKOUT

Discussion Groups (10 minutes)

Divide the group into two teams. Each team should research one half of the worksheet shown at the end of this session. Have each group choose a leader and a secretary. Distribute worksheets to everyone. Have group one research Section I and group two, Section II. Using their New Testaments, they should find the answers to the questions according to the specific references. After about seven minutes, bring everyone back together to report on their findings. The results should be as follows:

Jesus made some fantastic claims about Himself. These claims are recorded by original eyewitness sources. What were these claims? Jesus claimed:

1. to be God (John 10:30-33)
2. to be the only way to the Father (John 14:6)
3. to be the Son of God (Mark 14:61-62)
4. to have power to forgive sins (Mark 2:5-12)
5. to be the same as the Father (John 14:8-9)
6. that He fulfilled prophecy and existed before Abraham (John 8:51-58)

Jesus is from the beginning

Other people made statements about Jesus that help us understand Him. What did they say?

1. Jewish leaders accused Him of making Himself equal to God (John 5:18).
2. Martha: "I believe You are the Christ, the Son of God" (John 11:25-27).
3. Thomas: "My Lord and my God!" (John 20:25-28).
4. Peter: "The Christ, the Son of the living God" (Matthew 16:15-17).
5. Peter: Jesus never sinned, never told a lie, never answered back, suffered, personally carried our sins in His own body when He died on the cross, so we can be finished with sin. His wounds have healed ours (1 Peter 2:22-24).

Finish next week

WRAP-UP

Talk-to (5 minutes)

From our research we can see that *Jesus Christ is the God-Man*. The Gospels record Jesus' claims and those of His followers.

He was 100 percent God. He identified Himself with His Father; He accepted worship; He claimed certain powers that only God possesses— forgiving sins, casting out demons, raising the dead, knowing the future, etc.; He claimed eternal existence; and more.

He was 100 percent man. He was born; He experienced hunger; He knew pain; He had emotion; He reflected the dress and customs of His culture; etc.

Someone may say, "That's impossible! How can Jesus be both God and man at the same time? He must be one or the other." The answer is that certainly there's no way we can understand it completely; it is simply that the data only fits the category entitled "God-Man."

Remember that it takes time to move in and out of groups, so encourage everyone to move quickly to their places in the room.

During your talk, make specific references, when possible, to what has already been experienced and discussed.

In the scientific field, light is said to be made of "photons" which are "wave-particles." Someone can say, "That's impossible! How can light be both a 'wave' and a 'particle'?" The scientist only answers, "I have both sets of data; this demands the 'wave-particle' category."

Jesus is the Saviour. It is true that Jesus was the greatest moral Teacher who ever lived and that if you follow His way of life you will have mental health—but that's only a small part of the story. Jesus came to die and rise from the dead. He died for our sins; He took our place. Because of this, everyone is potentially "God's son."

Jesus now lives to give us a direct way to God. After we have established a personal relationship with Christ, through the Holy Spirit we can experience His day-by-day leading in our lives by yielding ourselves to Him.

If Jesus is not who He said He is, He must either be a lunatic or the world's greatest imposter. The evidence of a perfect life, hundreds of miracles and His personal resurrection seem to leave only one rational alternative. He *is* the God-Man.

Card Challenge (7 minutes)

Give everyone four, 3″ x 5″ cards, and make sure they have pencils or pens. At the bottom of each card have them write their names. Then, give them the following instructions.

Say something like: **During this session we have discovered four very important facts about Jesus. As I review these, I want you to write them on the top of your cards—one on each card. First, Jesus is 100 percent man; second, Jesus is 100 percent God; third, Jesus is the Saviour; fourth, Jesus is alive.**

Each of these facts should mean more to us than simply something to know about Jesus. They should apply directly to our relationships with God and how we live. Let me explain. "Jesus is 100 percent man" means that His suffering was real. When He hung on the cross, He was not putting on an act. He shed real blood and He died. And during His lifetime, He experienced all the human limitations and temptations that we do. Yet He didn't sin. Beneath the statement on this first card, write Hebrews 4:15-16. Because this is true, we know that Jesus truly understands us, no matter what we are experiencing, and we can talk to Him about anything.

The second statement reads, "Jesus is 100 percent God." This means that when Jesus died on the cross, He was not just another martyr, dying for a good cause. His death took care of the sin problem—the great barrier between us and God. Beneath the statement write Colossians 2:9. This also means that Jesus is the one reliable authority we can trust. His statements on life, death, morality, love, etc. are the final word. Our ideas must be measured by His.

"Jesus is the Saviour" is the third statement. This combines what I have just said about the first two statements concerning His death on the cross. The fact is, Jesus is the *only* way to God, and His death and Resurrection make this possible. Write Romans 5:6-11 beneath this statement. Jesus the Saviour died purposefully with you and me in mind. If His death were only an historical event, we could forget it. But we cannot ignore the Man who says He died for us by His own choice.

Our final statement is "Jesus is alive." He now lives and is interceding with

God on our behalf. Write Hebrews 7:25 beneath the statement. We must allow Him to guide us daily.

Encourage group members to look at their cards and honestly evaluate their own lives. Ask: **In which of these four areas is change needed? Are you totally honest with the God who knows you completely? Do you obey Christ; Is He your authority? Have you trusted Christ as your Saviour? Do you submit yourself to Christ's control daily?** Ask students to take the cards and their New Testaments and get alone with God. Each should choose the one card which is the most pertinent, look up the verse written on it, and spend a few moments in prayers about that need in his or her life.

Give group members time to conclude their silent prayers. Ask them to take all four cards home to refer to during the coming week.

After everyone has had a chance to pray, close by praying out loud.

Option for Further Study

Lead a group study (Sunday School class, small group, etc.) of the life Christ using *Who Is This Man Jesus?* This is a life of Christ in chronological order, taken from the Gospels.

Additional Resources

Who Is This Man Jesus? (H.S. Vigeveno, Regal Books)

More Than a Carpenter (Josh McDowell, Here's Life Publishers)
A close look at Jesus, His nature, character, and teachings. This is appropriate for leaders and students alike.

Following Jesus (Barry St. Clair, Victor Books)
A basic, inductive study for students on the fundamentals of knowing Christ.

JESUS WORKSHEET
Section I
JESUS ON JESUS: Jesus made some fantastic claims concerning who He is. What were actually some of His claims? Use the following statements from the original sources and summarize the significance of each statement on this sheet.

1. John 10:30-33
2. John 14:6
3. Mark 14:61-62
4. Mark 2:5-12
5. John 14:8-9
6. John 8:51-58

Section II
JESUS' CONTEMPORARIES ON JESUS: There are several ways to understand or know a person better. You can listen to what he says about himself, for example. Or you can see what others say about him. What did other people say about Jesus in the new Testament? Check out the statements listed here and summarize the significance of each comment on this sheet.

1. John 5:18
2. John 11:25-27 (Notice also what Jesus says about Himself)
3. John 20:25-28
4. Matthew 16:15-17
5. 1 Peter 2:22-24

SESSION 2

THE DECEIVER

Today we've going to talk about WHO IS THE DEVIL, AND HOW CAN HE BE DEFEATED?

KEY CONCEPT

We must remember always that Satan is real and must be taken seriously. It is also true, however, that he can be defeated through Jesus Christ.

GOAL

This session will help your young people investigate the person of Satan as described in the Bible and how he is defeated in the life of the Christian by Jesus Christ.

OVERVIEW

Today as never before, occult practices are gaining widespread acceptance in society. Supernatural power is featured in television shows from children's cartoons to situation comedies, and the movie page is packed with occult "thrillers." This exposure leads many young people to be attracted to the powers of darkness and to experiment in various occult practices. On the other hand, there is little respect for the *real* power of Satan and the results of following him. He is usually pictured wearing red flannel underwear, having horns, and carrying a pitchfork. That kind of devil is not taken very seriously. But Satan is real and must not be ignored or toyed with. This session, therefore, will take a close look at the biblical description of the devil and his power and will emphasize the reality of our victory through Christ over him.

TIME REQUIRED

30-45 minutes

MATERIALS CHECKLIST

Materials needed for basic session:

____ Stories *(Rumbling Rumors)*
____ Quizzes *(Great Liars of History)*
____ *Satan Identified* worksheets
____ Pencils or pens

____ Bibles
____ Person to play "the deceiver"
____ Poster board or chalk
____ Blank paper *(Gaps in the Armor)*

Materials needed for optional activities:
____ People and stories *(To Tell The Truth)*
____ Materials for *Spot the Phonies* (See suggestions listed with that activity.)
____ A copy of The *Screwtape Letters* by C.S. Lewis

JUNIOR HIGH ADAPTATION

This is an important session for junior highers, but the research section could move a little slowly for them. Either cut down the number of verses they have to look up or have an adult helper read some of them out loud for each small group. Also, *Rumbling Rumors* and *Great Liars of History* should be written with their age in mind (e.g. How many remember Nixon?). Finally, during the *Wrap-up,* use specific illustrations from their lives to emphasize each point.

WARM-UP

Optional Openers

To Tell The Truth (12 minutes)

Beforehand, select three young people and get together to plan this activity. Find one thing that one of them has done or one unique characteristic that is unlikely to be true of any other person in the group (e.g. climbed a mountain, all-star little league pitcher, born in Africa, etc.) and that most of them do not know about. Have that person tell the other two as many of the details as possible. Write up a short account of that experience, and select one phrase that all the contestants can use to make the claim for themselves.

When the group meets, announce that you are going to play "To Tell the Truth." It will be a test to see how good they are at separating truth from error. Introduce the three participants and assign them numbers. Explain that one of them has a unique charac- teristic and that group members should try to pick the "real" person by questioning all three. One must tell the truth—the other two will "lie" as convincingly as possible.

Have each participant stand and repeat the agreed on phrase. Read the prepared statement and let the audience ask questions, directing each question to either #1, #2, or #3. After about ten minutes, vote on the truth teller. Have a few students explain why they chose a particular person. Finally, end the suspense by saying: **Will the real_____ please stand up?** You may have that person relate some interesting details on his or her unique experience.

Spot the Phonies (6 minutes)

Collect a number of "copies" of originals. Bring the copies and the originals (if possible) and hold them up one at a time in front of the group. They are to decide which items are phony and which ones are the genuine articles. Here are some possibilities:

 1. print of a painting
 2. photocopy of a document
 3. forgery of the signature of a famous person
 4. "look-alike" product, copy of a name brand
 5. "cola-looking" liquid in a coke bottle
 6. "candy bar" sticker
 7. plastic or silk flower
 8. "classic" book cover covering another book
 9. plastic egg
10. voice impression of a famous person (on tape)

Be sure to mix the genuine with the fake. After displaying all the items and voting, ask group members what they would do *next* to determine the "truth" of each one. This will vary according to the item, from touch or taste to a closer look, etc. Ask for examples of when group members have been fooled, how they felt, what difference it made in their lives.

The Screwtape Letters (5 minutes)

Use this classic book by C.S. Lewis as a dramatic reading. Have two students read a couple of letters and the responses, then discuss the nature of Satan's subtle attacks on Christians.

Advance preparation is very important for the success of this activity. Make sure that your "contestants" are well-rehearsed. The goal of this is to have fun and to highlight the difficulty of determining who is telling the truth.

The idea here is to highlight counter-feits and how it is often very difficult to determine which is the genuine article.

This would fit best after *Great Liars of History* or *Group Research.*

The Deceiver

This may be difficult to do with a junior higher. With any group, however, selecting the right person is critical. He or she must not be someone perceived as a "joker" or "troublemaker." The point is to surprise everyone when he or she is identified. The parallel is of Satan as an attractive, deceiving, "angel of light."

Beforehand, choose one of the group members to be an undercover "deceiver." In other words, this person should try to convince other group members to choose wrong answers, not follow directions, cheat, and/or find wrong concepts in the Bible. Choose this person carefully because he or she must be well liked by the group and able to be convincing. He or she should choose the "deceiving times" well. After *Group Research,* he or she should be "unmasked" and the experience discussed.

Rumbling Rumors (5 minutes)

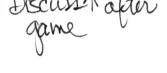
Peter Piper Picked Peck of Pickled

"Telephone" —

This activity is not "deception," but it does show how messages can be twisted and distorted. If you do this as a whole group, make sure the "deceiver" does not interfere—the message will be twisted very naturally.

Discuss after game

This can be done in teams or in one group. Type out a short story (or one for each team) of about 25 words using a lot of descriptive adjectives. Have everyone in each team or the whole group form a single-file line (while seated). Now, give the story to the first person in line. He or she must read it and then repeat it verbally, without consulting the paper, to the next person, whispering it in his or her ear. This person then whispers the story to the next person and so on until they get to the end of the line. When the last person has heard the story, have him or her tell the entire group what he or she heard. Then read the original to show how mixed-up the story became.

Great Liars of History (5 minutes)

~~She Shell~~ She sell shells by

Some of these may be too difficult for your group or "dated" (e.g. Leonid Brezhnev). Add others from recent news events.

Distribute the following matching quiz. Add other more contemporary or applicable examples. They should match the "lie" with the "liar." The correct answers have been placed in parentheses for your benefit.

____ the serpent in Eden (e)
____ Leonid Brezhnev (i)
____ Abraham (a)
____ Fidel Castro (h)

____ Jacob (f)
____ Ananias (d)
____ Georgia Pacific Co. (g)
____ Cain (b)
____ Ayatollah Khomeini (j)
____ Peter (c)

a. "She is my sister."
b. "Am I my brother's keeper?"
c. "I never knew Him."
d. "This is all the money we received from our property."
e. "You will *not* surely die."
f. "I am the oldest son."
g. "What chemical spill?"
h. "What missiles?"
i. "What invasion?"
j. "What hostages?"

Give the correct answers and acknowledge the person(s) with the most right. Then, go immediately into the discussion.

Discussion (5 minutes)

This discussion should serve as a transition, so make sure it moves quickly.

Ask: **What have our activities, so far, had in common?** They were about twisted messages, deception, and lies.) **What people or situations are usually associated with lies and lying?** (Group members may mention salesmen, politicians, cult leaders, etc.)
Why? (They want to get something from us—money, votes, etc.)
Where do lies originate? (Our sinful nature, Satan) **Why is Satan called the "father of lies"?** (Lies grow out of the evil Satan is responsible for.) **What do most people think of the devil?** (Many people don't believe in him. A few worship him.) **Is Satan real? How do you know?** (Discuss answers. Move into next section for a deeper look at the reality and nature of Satan.)

WORKOUT

Say something like: **The Bible says Satan is real and gives a description of him. Right now we're going to learn all we can about what Scripture teaches about Satan.** ~~Let's get into groups of five or six to research Satan and his work.~~ *Hand out worksheets*

Group Research (10 minutes)

Distribute to small groups copies of the worksheet "Satan Identified" without answers (printed at the end of the session) and divide the Scripture passages among the groups. Have them discuss the verses and complete the worksheet for their specific verses. They should list the titles of Satan, describe his purpose if mentioned in each passage, and explain how he accomplishes his work. After the groups finish, come back together as one group and list all findings on a poster board or chalkboard. As you go along, probe to be sure the young people understand the implications of the various titles given to Satan. Discuss briefly how his methods affect each of us.

Remember, it takes time to move into and out of small groups. Make sure everyone moves quickly, forming groups right where they sit. The reporting phase should take half of your allotted time.

Deceiver Identified (5 minutes)

Up until this point your planted "deceiver" has been undercover, confusing the issue and trying to lead group members astray. Now is the time to let everyone in on the secret. Have the person come to the front of the room and explain his or her role. Then ask this person how successful he or she was and what he or she used to try to deceive others in each of the activities. Ask group members how they felt when they were being "persuaded" by the "deceiver" and how they decided whether or not to believe him or her. Referring to their worksheets, emphasize the fact that Satan is pictured as an "angel of light," as sneaky as a serpent, and as a liar and deceiver. Ask how they think Satan might try to deceive them. Would he be obvious? Attractive? Easy to resist on our own? Etc. Then, move into your *Talk-to*.

When you identify the "deceiver," build him or her in the eyes of the group, thanking him or her for doing a great job and for being a great sport.

WRAP-UP

Talk-to (5 minutes)

We've identified who Satan is and what he does, but where did he come from and where is he going? We know that God created all things, but would He create an evil being? The Bible tells us that Satan was originally good. He was known as Lucifer, the "son of the morning," but he tried to usurp God's power, and he fell. He became God's enemy by his own choice. Read Isaiah 14:9-17.

Satan's end is clearly foretold in the Bible too. The verses I just read say that his destiny is hell—eternal separation from God. The last book in the Bible, Revelation, also tells about his future. Read Revelation 20:1-3, 10.

Satan is indeed real. He is powerful. He is our enemy. And those of us who know Jesus Christ have some wonderful resources available to us in the battle.

Jesus Christ, by His own death and resurrection, has defeated Satan. We are told in Philippians 2:9-11 of His ultimate victory when all will bow at His feet. Read Philippians 2:9-11. **Jesus Christ provides us with the spiritual armor to defeat Satan.** Read Ephesians 6:10-18. **When we resist Satan, he will leave us.** Read James 4:7. **We can expect problems, but we are victorious because Jesus' power is available to us.** Read 1 John 4:4 and Romans 8:35-39.

Make sure you have the Bible verses marked to save time.

As they write, give suggestions concerning the "lies" and their "gaps." It would be helpful to ask for reports on students' progress the next week.

In summary, Satan was created by God—a powerful angel who sought God's throne—and was banished by God. He is now God's archenemy. He moves through the world attempting to defeat God's purpose. He has access to God. His power is limited by God. The believer in Christ is secure from Satan's power. Satan will one day be totally defeated and thrown into eternal hell.

Gaps in the Armor (10 minutes)

Distribute blank pieces of paper to everyone. Tell them to write down as many of Satan's current lies as they can think of. These can be cultural values ("look out for #1, "if it feels good, do it," etc.), ideas they have heard at school ("popularity is very important," "how a person looks means more than what he is like on the inside," etc.), values presented in television shows ("life is cheap," "sex is everything," etc.), and other thoughts and ideas. Then have them analyze their lives, identifying areas where they could be susceptible to Satan's attacks through lies, pressure, etc., especially in light of the lies written above. They should write these areas on their sheets. As they write, offer suggestions to stimulate their thinking ("What about your values . . . what's important to you?", "How's your dating life?", "What's your attitude toward money?", etc.)

Next, have group members choose the one area where they are probably most vulnerable. Tell them to write a three-step strategy for dealing with this problem or weakness. The steps could include prayer, telling someone else, asking for counsel, reading, and others. Challenge them to take their papers with them, to put into practice those action steps, and to ask God for guidance and help in the other "gap" areas.

Option for Further Study

Purchase the InterVarsity booklets, *The Occult* by Brooks Alexander, and make them available for everyone. This is a very concise and helpful discussion of occult practices, their nature and dangers.

Additional Resources

The Occult (Brooks Alexander, InterVarsity Press)

The Screwtape Letters (C.S. Lewis, The Macmillan Company)
Lewis' most well known work, this classic volume is a collection of fictional letters written from a senior to a junior devil. It contains profound insights into human nature and the wiles of the devil.

Satan is Alive and Well on Planet Earth (Hal Lindsey, Zondervan)
A helpful analysis of Satan's influence in contemporary culture.

WORKSHEET — SATAN IDENTIFIED

SCRIPTURE	TITLE	PURPOSE	METHOD
2 Cor. 4:4	God of evil world	Keep people from the Gospel	Blinds people
Eph. 2:2	Mighty prince of power of the air	Against the Lord	Works in hearts Pressures conformity
1 Peter 5:8	Great enemy Roaring Lion		Attacks ruthlessly
Matt. 4:1-11	Satan	To tempt Christ	Strike in weakness Question identity Misquote Scripture Sensational appeal Appeal to pride Shortcut God's plan
2 Cor. 11:14	Satan Angel of Light	Deceive	Appear attractive
John 8:44	Devil, Murderer Hater of Truth Father of Liars	Deceive, Destroy	Lie
Gen. 3:1-13	Serpent		Question God's Words Appeal of pride
1 Tim. 4:1-4		Turn people away from Christ	Inspire lying teachers who appear good
Matt. 24:24		Deceive God's chosen ones	False prophets False Christs
Matt. 13:24-30; 13:36-43	Satan, Devil, enemy	Hurt the people of Christ	Live among Christians
James 3:15-16	Devil	Cause Disorder	Inspire jealousy, selfishness
Col. 1:13	Satan	Enslave in darkness	
Job 1:6-12; 2:4-6	Satan	Tempt Job to curse God	Take possessions Take health

SESSION 3

ALL OF ME

HAVE I GIVEN MY *WHOLE* LIFE TO CHRIST?

KEY CONCEPT

Often Christians put God "in a box," limiting His lordship to one area of life.

GOAL

This session will challenge your young people to allow Christ to bring growth and maturity to all areas of their lives.

OVERVIEW

When we become Christians, we give our lives to Christ. In reality, however, we often tend to limit Him to certain areas (such as the spiritual) or specific situations (such as church, witnessing). But Christ must be "Lord *of* all" if He is to be "Lord *at* all." In other words, we must allow Him to invade every area of our lives: physical, social, mental, and spiritual. There is also the tendency to become "out of balance in our lives," emphasizing one or two areas and totally ignoring the rest. When this happens, we become lopsided and ineffective in our service for Christ. Jesus wants to make us whole, and He wants whole people to serve Him. This session, therefore, will focus attention on each of the four major life-areas of young people and challenge them to make necessary changes.

TIME REQUIRED

30-45 minutes

MATERIALS CHECKLIST

Materials needed for basic session:
____ Old magazines and grocery bags *(Thoughts)*
____ *On My Mind* worksheets
____ Pencils or pens and paper for everyone
____ New Testaments

Materials for optional activities:
____ Rubber bands (*Rubber Band Race*)
____ Saltine crackers and soft drinks (*Burp and Whistle*)
____ Prizes for winners of *Warm-up* activities

JUNIOR HIGH ADAPTATION

This session will be very helpful for junior highers because they are undergoing so many changes in all areas of their lives. In fact, you may want to spend extended time in each area and spread this material over two sessions. Because of these changes and pressures, your junior highers probably will not want to openly discuss what they really think, especially in the physical and social areas; so don't try to force discussion. Instead, summarize and move on. Also, as written, the *Optional Openers* would not be good for junior highers unless they are quite secure socially. Adapt these activities for your group. For example, have a pop-drinking contest instead of *Burp and Whistle*.

WARM-UP

Optional Openers

Rubber Band Race (5 minutes)

Choose three contestants or ask for three volunteers (preferably boys or girls with short hair). Place a thick rubber band around the head and over the tip of the nose of each contestant. At your signal, they must race to see who can maneuver the rubber band down off the nose to the neck. Any facial contortion is legal, but they may not use their hands or any other part of the body or rub against anything else.

Burp and Whistle (5 minutes)

Choose two or three couples to compete. Give each boy five saltine crackers and his girl partner a carbonated soft drink. At your signal they should all begin to eat and drink. The first couple whose boy can get all the saltines into his mouth and whistle and whose girl can drink her soft drink and then burp, wins.

Thoughts (8 minutes)

Give each student a grocery bag. Tell them to fill their bags with pictures torn from magazines and newspaper stacked in the center of the room. The pictures are to represent "thoughts recently on my mind." After about five minutes, stop and have some or all of them share, one at a time, what is in their bags and why.

On My Mind (7 minutes)

Give piece of paper, write down thoughts [handwritten]

Distribute the *On My Mind* worksheets (printed at end of session). Say something like: **Here's a sheet that includes all sorts of things that you've already mentioned plus some others that kids are thinking about. Some of these will really get to the core of what's been on your mind lately. Let's take a look at "Acceptance and Popularity," for example. When I was in high school, I vividly remember how important it was to me to be noticed by the right people. If I walked down the hall and certain people didn't say hello, I was absolutely devastated.** (You can adapt these statements to generalize them if necessary.) **Or how about the area of 'Desires?' I can remember feeling guilty about _____ and just about cracking up under the pressure. I think some of you go through the same agony I went through—you know what I'm talking about. A sheet like this helps us sort out our feelings and thoughts. Now you don't have to do if you don't want to—but if you do, please be honest. Extend, into the center, the arrows of those things that have been on your mind lately. In other words, what are the areas that concern you most, right now? We do this to help us get an overview of what makes up our total lives.**

Explain that they will notice that one or two of the four major areas standout as more important than others. On some they used lots of arrows; others they left untouched. Ask: **Who had most, or quite a few, arrows coming from the physical area? How about the mental area? Social? Religious or spiritual? If your arrows were the spokes of a wheel, how would your wheel look? Balanced? Unbalanced?** Point out that our lives will run about the same way. If we are lopsided or way out of balance, we will experience great difficulty in those areas where we have virtually nothing.

This is a "physical" activity whose purpose is to have fun and to relax the group. Make sure you choose participants who won't mind looking a little foolish in front of the others. Afterward, congratulate all of the contestants for being "good sports."

The purpose of this activity is to have fun and to focus on the "physical" area of life. When the boys try to whistle, they may blow a few crackers on the audience, so be prepared. Make sure you thank *all* the contestants for their participation.

Make sure they understand what you want to do, and then move the activity along. You want to have time for them to display and explain their "thoughts." The purpose of this activity is to focus on their recent major concerns and to set the stage for *On My Mind.*

Press the reality of these worries as hard as you have to in order to make sure the crowd is taking them seriously, not just on the surface.

Allow time to draw arrows.

Priorities (5 minutes)

Be sure to give examples.

Pass out paper and pencils for group members to take notes as you brainstorm a list of possible priorities in each area of life—spiritual, physical, social, and mental. Examples might include: church, Bible study, evangelism, appearance, dating, sports, popularity, fun, friends, grades, desires, etc. Next, each person should evaluate each of these things and list the top eight items in order of personal priority. Encourage them to be totally honest.

Allow time to write. As they work, remind students that there are no "right" answers. There's no audience for them to impress, so if they list them out of order just to look good, they're fooling only themselves.

WORKOUT

Discussion (7 minutes)

Some young people may say, "Well, He should be number one" or "Yes, I put Bible Study and Prayer near the top." That is not really the solution, because that compartmentalizes God (and they are probably giving those answers because they think you want them).

Ask: **How does God fit in with your list of priorities?**

Listen to and interact with their answers, and then say something like: **Well, I don't think we're very clear on how this all fits together. God is not nearly as interested in being just one more item in our lives as He is in affecting all the items. Let's look at how Jesus developed in His relationship with God when He was on earth.**

This is a transition, so make sure it doesn't bog down.

Read and discuss Luke 2:52, the only biblical description of Christ's teenage years; also Luke 2:40, Philippians 2:5-13; and Hebrews 5:5-9. Ask what they think Jesus was like as a teenager, mentally, spiritually, socially, and physically. Discuss how this information relates to them and how they think they should respond.

Talk-to (3 minutes)

Jesus grew by obedience. He applied the values (words, principles, teachings, attitudes) that His Father showed Him to His own life. He studied and memorized the Scriptures just as we do. He prayed to His Father in the same way we do. The only difference was that He was able to maintain a perfect attitude in all situations.

But that doesn't disqualify Him from being our pattern. His attitudes (what He thought and felt) affected His actions (what He did) which determined His accomplishments (what He achieved). In the same way, we can let His attitudes affect _our_ attitudes, which will determine our actions and accomplishments. Jesus developed as a whole Person; the aspects of His life were all integrated (in other words, He was "together") under the leadership of His Father. He showed us, both in action and in word, how God can affect every corner of our lives.

Adjustments (7 minutes)

Be sure to give examples.

Say something like: **Take a little time now and stare at your worksheet entitled "Priorities: What's Important?" Try to imagine what God would do if He were allowed to get involved in the first priority on your list, or the second, or third. Then start making notes to yourself on your papers about** things you'd like to realign or change, ways in which God relates to your concerns, etc. Some of these will be easy to spot; others will be difficult and may require a lot of struggle, prayer, and counseling.

WRAP-UP

Talk-to (3 minutes)

As you can tell, we're talking about something very basic and very far-reaching. We're talking about the fundamental nature of the Christan life, which is growth. I can't think of a more important concept than this one: moving toward maturity in Christ. Listen to these verses:

Read 2 Peter 3:18; Ephesians 4:15; 2 Peter 1:8-9, then say something like: **If we don't keep on growing as Christians, we become stunted in our growth. The Christian's long-range goal must always be to conform to Jesus, whose grasp of whole-person development is the best. That's why Romans 8:29 says, "For those God foreknew He also predestined to be conformed to the likeness of His Son, that He might be the firstborn among many brothers." We look forward to the day when "we shall be like Him, for we shall see Him as He is" (1 John 3:2).**

Other Scriptures with the same idea: Ephesians 1:9-12 and Philippians 1:20-21.

In the meantime, what is the Christian's short-range goal? To live each day, a day at a time, in openness and obedience to what Christ is showing us. The listing on these sheets can help you analyze how you're doing and know whether you've committed all you know about these various areas to Christ.

Accountability (5 minutes)

Have everyone find a partner whom they know fairly well. Next, have them share one or two of the adjustments on their sheets about which they are concerned and they will be praying. Close by having them pray for each other as they make these necessary adjustments. Challenge them to keep in touch over the next few weeks to check on each other's progress.

It will take time for them to find partners. Help them get together quickly and encourage them to take this very seriously.

Options for Further Study

Offer various options for those who need special help in certain areas: for example, tutoring or a seminar on "How to Study" for the mental area; aerobic exercising, jogging, etc. for the physical; discussions on relationships and/or dating for the social; and a group to design a worship experience for the spiritual.

A good follow-up to this session is session 8 in this book. It deals with putting God at the center of life.

Additional Resources

Celebration of Discipline (Richard Foster, Harper and Row)
A practical discussion of the spiritual disciplines, this book would be very helpful for your more mature young people.

100% . . . Beyond Mediocrity (Fred Hartley, Revell)
A challenge to total commitment, this book covers the basics of real Christian growth.

ON MY MIND

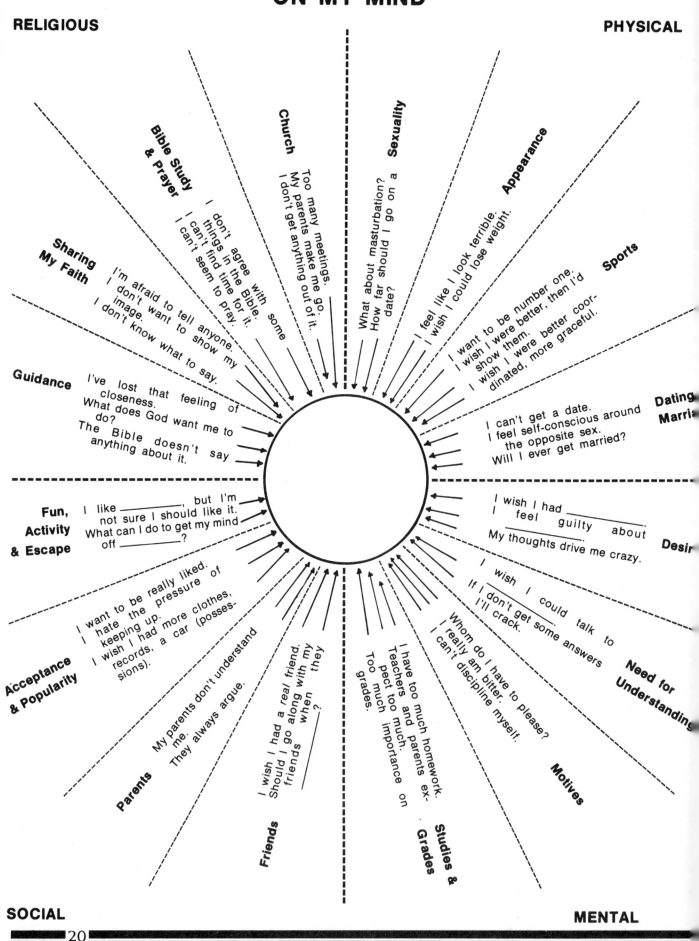

RELIGIOUS

PHYSICAL

Bible Study & Prayer
I don't agree with some things in the Bible.
I can't find time for it.
I can't seem to pray.

Church
Too many meetings.
My parents make me go.
I don't get anything out of it.

Sexuality
What about masturbation?
How far should I go on a date?

Appearance
I feel like I look terrible.
I wish I could lose weight.

Sharing My Faith
I'm afraid to tell anyone.
I don't want to show my image.
I don't know what to say.

Sports
I want to be number one.
I wish I were better, then I'd show them.
I wish I were better coordinated, more graceful.

Guidance
I've lost that feeling of closeness.
What does God want me to do?
The Bible doesn't say anything about it.

Dating & Marriage
I can't get a date.
I feel self-conscious around the opposite sex.
Will I ever get married?

Fun, Activity & Escape
I like _____, but I'm not sure I should like it.
What can I do to get my mind off _____?

Desire
I wish I had _____
I feel guilty about _____
My thoughts drive me crazy.

Acceptance & Popularity
I want to be really liked.
I hate the pressure of keeping up.
I wish I had more clothes, records, a car (possessions).

Need for Understanding
I wish I could talk to _____
If I don't get some answers I'll crack.

Parents
My parents don't understand me.
They always argue.

Motives
Whom do I have to please?
Who really am I bitter?
I can't discipline myself.

Friends
I wish I had a real friend.
Should I go along with my friends when they _____?

Studies & Grades
I have too much homework.
Teachers and parents expect too much.
Too much importance on grades.

SOCIAL

MENTAL

20

SESSION 4

GOD'S FOREVER FAMILY

HOW IMPORTANT IS THE CHURCH?

KEY CONCEPT

Many young people lack a real understanding and appreciation of the church (the body of Christ) and churches in general.

GOAL

This session will emphasize how God's family (the church) today comes together in church. It will lead your young people to see how churches began, what they should be like, why they are important, and how to be a creative part of them.

OVERVIEW

It is easy to "take the church for granted," attending Sunday after Sunday without really understanding its purpose and importance in our lives. Young people are especially susceptible to this because they are usually taken to church (not necessarily by their own choice) and do not occupy leadership positions within the church. If they do not become involved in the life of the church or learn about its importance for their lives, they will probably "leave the church" when they leave home. But church should be a vital part of the life of every Christian, as the collected assembly of "Christ's body," the place for fellowship and worship, and the source of spiritual instruction and motivation. This session, therefore, will explain the purpose of the church and challenge young people to make church an integral part of their lives, now and in the future.

TIME REQUIRED

30–45 minutes

MATERIALS CHECKLIST

Materials needed for basic session:
_____ Pencils or pens for everyone
_____ Cards for *Quiz*
_____ New Testaments
_____ Chalkboard and chalk or flip chart and markers
_____ Blank pieces of paper (*Strategy*)

Materials needed for optional activities:
_____ Special guest (*Vocational Guidance*)
_____ Labels and names (*Famous People*)

JUNIOR HIGH ADAPTATION

It is important for junior highers to begin to think through the whole concept of the church, and the session may be used as it is written with the following modifications: During the Bible study, don't break into groups. Instead, have selected individuals read aloud the passages. After each one, summarize the message for them.

WARM-UP

Optional Openers

Famous People (7 minutes)

As students enter the room, slap a sticky label onto their backs bearing the names of famous people from the Bible and church history (such as Moses, John Calvin, Gideon, Francis Schaffer, Esther, Hudson Taylor, Deborah, Ruth, Billy Sunday, Adam, Balaam, Lot, Sarah, Billy Graham, D.L. Moody, Abel, Stephen, Martin Luther, Barnabas, Matthew, Chuck Swindoll, Abigail, etc.). Make sure that all mirrors are removed from the room and that all reflecting windows are covered with drapery. Explain that the object of the game is to find out "who you are" by asking questions of the others in the room. They can only ask each person two questions, and the questions must be answered by "yes" or "no." When they think they know their identities, they should come to you for confirmation.

Vocational Guidance (8 minutes)

Line-up a pastor from another church and introduce him/her as a special guest who will help them with choosing their careers. Explain that you don't want to tell them directly what the occupation is, but they can try to find out through questions. Begin by asking:

1. Why did you choose this career?
2. What do you like most about your job?
3. What do you dislike most about your job?
4. Why do you think your vocation is necessary in the world?
5. How do you know when you have done your job well?

Next, let everyone else ask questions. After a few minutes, see who can guess your guest's occupation and then introduce him/her. He or she could stay for the whole session and comment at the end on "the most meaningful aspect of church for me as a pastor."

Discussion (5 minutes)

Make sure everyone is seated and that you have their attention; then say something like: **Imagine that you've just moved to another state, and you know of no Christian youth group like ours. There's nothing happening spiritually on your new campus. What do you do if . . .**
- you develop problems in your relationship with God; you've stopped growing, and you know it?
- you need Christian friends and you can't find any?
- you need answers from the Bible and you don't know where to look? (Discuss briefly—don't mention church until a student does.)

Talk-to (3 minutes)

Wherever you go throughout your life as a Christian, you'll carry two needs with you: (1) the need to be fed spiritually, and (2) the need to be with other Christians. Our youth group can help meet those two needs during high school (or junior high), but what about college? The military? When you're married? Employed? Where do you find God's family?

The purpose of this game is to have fun and to center everyone's thoughts around great men and women of the church. Don't wait too long to begin. Start the game right after you explain the rules and distribute the labels.

Make sure that this person is a "stranger" to your group. Brief him or her thoroughly in advance concerning your questions and expectations. Explain that he or she should not give away the "occupation" with his or her answers.

This discussion is an introduction, so don't spend too much time on it or let it drag.

The Christian life was never meant to be lived alone. It's a family affair. Jesus started it with an intimate group of 12 who got excited about His teaching and the fellowship of understanding it together. But how could Jesus guarantee that all Christians everywhere would share His spiritual family experience? He started the idea of the church—the ongoing family of Jesus.

Quiz (8 minutes)

Right now some of you are thinking, *Wow—what happened to Jesus' idea? Something sure got messed up somewhere along the line.* Most people get their ideas of what church is from modern religion, not the Bible.

Hand out index cards and pencils. Have group members write their answers to this true-false quiz on concepts about churches.

1. Churches were started by early Christians to keep Christianity alive. (False)
2. Churches should be made up of people who are trying to find God. (False)
3. Not every "church on the corner" is what Jesus would call a church. (True)
4. The main purpose of a church should be to provide a wholesome climate for the community. (False)
5. By the New Testament definition, our youth group could be called a "church." (False)
6. All members of local churches are Christians. (False)
7. A Christian should try to get his or her most serious problems straightened out before he or she gets involved in a church. (False)
8. From what we can tell about churches in the New Testatment, it's a good idea to separate Christians by age-groups. (False)
9. The church building has virtually nothing to do with the real church. (True)
10. A Christian can accomplish what a church does simply by being alone with the Lord. (False)

WORKOUT

Talk-to (5 minutes)

As you give the following points, write them on the board. Say something like: **Some Christians have been poor, some rich; some live in China, some in Chile, some in Chicago. Some are being persecuted violently while others are praised. Nineteen hundred years ago they hid in caves under Rome; today they dress up for a weekly appearance in an air-conditioned building.**

But Jesus knew that "family time" would always be needed because of three unchanging factors:

1. *What the world is like.* It's naturally hostile toward God and anyone who tries to live for Him. Christians are always a minority under fire. They need to band together.

2. *What the Bible is like.* It's God's revelation of Himself; therefore, it's heavy stuff! Christians always need the help of others who have really studied it to help them understand and use it properly.

3. *What humans are like.* We don't function very well alone. We have an instinctive need to be with people who support us. Alone, we shrivel up; together, we grow.

Read the questions out loud while they write their answers on the cards.

Go back and give them the correct answers (in parentheses). They may argue with you, but don't stop to prove or disprove anything now. Instead, note which questions were unanimous and which had significant disagreement.

Encourage them to record these three main points on the backs of their cards.

Because you and I live in a hostile world, need to understand the Bible, and are interdependent, we need the church wherever it is today. But what is a "Jesus-church" like? Looking at all the denominations, you could get the idea that nobody really knows. The only reliable description is in the Bible. If we're going to find the real church in our world, we're going to have to find out what to look for.

Bible Study (10 minutes)

Break into three groups and give them the following worksheet and the assignment to read the section of verses and to report about what they learned about the church from them. Assign passages 1 and 2 to group #1; 3 and 4 to group 2; and 5 and 6 to group 3.

1. Matthew 16:18 (Who started the church? Who can stop it?)
2. Acts 2:41-46 (What's the qualification for being in the church? What happens in a church? The church is not a bunch of people trying to find God; it's people who already have. They are together because they know Christ. They come together for teaching by someone who's trained, sharing of the Lord's Supper, praying, sharing needs and joys, helping the needy, and worshiping.)
3. Colossians 1:18; Ephesians 2:20-22 (What does this tell you about your relationship to every other Christian? There's an invisible glue between us all. We belong to each other because we all belong to Jesus. We're God's forever family.)
4. Hebrews 10:25 (Is the church just an invisible relationship? No, it takes regular, visible form in a local meeting.)
5. 1 Timothy 3:1-2, 8, 15 (Is the church just a loose, informal discussion group? No, it meets as an organized group, with designated leaders. This is to make sure we get good teaching and accomplish our goals.)
6. Titus 2:2-6 (Why not a teenage church? Because we need to include all age-groups.)

After a few minutes, gather everyone back together and have the groups report. Encourage everyone to record the answers from the other groups on their worksheets, and list on the board the characteristics of a church. The list should read something like this:

Jesus' idea
People who are together because they know Christ
Invisible relationship
Visible get-togethers
Organized
All ages, etc.

WRAP-UP

Talk-to (6 minutes)

Say something like: **So God's family is still alive and well and to be found in local bodies of believers. A Christian without a church is missing an essential part of his or her life in Christ. What good is it to be part of a family you're never with? When you find a real church in any community, you have found God's people—including spiritual fathers who will try to feed you the balanced diet you need to grow.**

Remember, it takes time to break into and come out of groups; therefore, have them form three groups with a minimum of movement. Appoint a discussion leader for each group. If they finish early, encourage them to move to another section. As the answers are given, be sure to refer back to the *Quiz* whenever appropriate.

Discussion questions and answers are in parentheses. Use these to prod their thinking during the reports.

Let me close by giving you a few hints: Since churches are people, no church is perfect. You'll miss a lot of spiritual help if you wait to find the perfect church. Remember, God is still building all those other Christians just like He's building you. It's because we're all growing and struggling that we need each other so much.

Take advantage of what a church is and help to make it what it isn't. Get the fellowship and spiritual food, and provide fellowship for some of the others there who need you.

Get regular input from a real church throughout your life. Right now you may be attending a specific church because of your parents. Eventually you will have to choose a church for yourself, either here or in another city. When choosing a church, make sure you look for one where the Bible and Christ are the center of activity.

You get out of church what you put into it. Our youth group isn't church; it's not meant to be. And church isn't a youth group—it's not meant for entertainment. You have to listen, become involved in the worship experience, take notes, and really put yourself into it to get the most out of it.

You need your spiritual family . . . and they need you. You're incomplete without each other. If you haven't already started, begin right now to build a life habit of being with your forever family.

Strategy (5 minutes)

Distribute blank pieces of paper and have group members answer the following two questions:

1. Remember our opening discussion about your move to a new town? Now, after all we've learned in this session, what would you do to find fellowship, growth, or problem-solving? Design a brief strategy.

2. What can you do to become more involved in church right now? Design a brief strategy.

Encourage group members to keep their strategies in their Bibles and remember to pray about them.

Encourage them to talk to you or the other leaders about their "strategies." Also, if a number of them are interested in worship, have them plan a service for the whole group.

Option for Further Study

Hold a special seminar on the distinctives of your church (taught by the pastor or another church leader).

Additional Resources

Worship (Ronald Allen and Gordon Borror, Multnomah)
A thorough and practical analysis of worship, this book would be good reading for both adult and student leaders and could form the basis for planning a worship service together.

You and Your Network (Fred Smith, Word)
Though this is not specifically about the church, it focuses on our need to learn from and relate to others. Obviously your church should be a vital part of your interpersonal network.

SESSION 5

I AM SOMEBODY

WHO AM I?

KEY CONCEPT	Most young people struggle with their self-concepts (identity), feeling virtually "worthless" much of the time.
GOAL	This session will help each of your young people see that he or she is a unique creation of God—a person for whom Christ died and whom God loves, with infinite value and worth.
OVERVIEW	The critical focus of young people during adolescence is "identity"—who they are and where they fit in. Because of this, they are susceptible to peer pressure, cliques, and all sorts of internal pressures. A solid, positive self-concept begins with self-worth—feeling good about oneself. Too often, however, the opposite is true. Experiences of failure, ridicule, and inadequacy foster the idea that "I am nobody very special" or "I am a poor excuse for a person." But the truth is that every person is loved by *God,* is valuable to Him, and can be used by Him. Understanding this truth can revolutionize a young person's life; for when a person can accept and "love" him/herself, he or she will be free to love others. This session will emphasize the reality of God's infinite love for each young person and will challenge them to build a realistic view of themselves based on this fact.
TIME REQUIRED	30-45 minutes
MATERIALS CHECKLIST	Materials needed for basic session: ____ Paper (*Who are You?*) ____ Pencils or pens ____ New Testaments ____ Worksheets (*Bible Search*) ____ Printed copies of Psalm 139 Materials needed for optional activities: ____ Questions (*Happy Hobbies*) ____ The movie *Claude* or *Eagle Beak*, projector, and screen
JUNIOR HIGH ADAPTATION	Most of the session can be used as it is with these changes: do not use *Happy Hobbies*; use *Hey Simpson*, but do not use the optional verse; during the discussion, simplify and shorten the questions; during the *Bible Search*, work on the verses together instead of breaking into groups.

WARM-UP

Optional Opener

Happy Hobbies (10 minutes)

Send four or five guys out of the room. Tell them you are going to ask them questions about their hobbies, but they are not to identify their hobbies. Instead, the audience will try to guess what they are.

While they are out of the room, tell (or have another leader tell) the audience that the guys think that they will be talking about their hobbies, but actually they will be answering questions about kissing!

Bring them all into the room and ask them all question #1; then ask them question #2, etc. Here are the questions:

1. How old were you when you first did this?
2. Who taught you how?
3. Is there someone with whom you really like to do this?
4. Where do you usually practice this?
5. Is there a particular time of day you like to do this?
6. When you do this, what kind of sound does it make?
7. With how many people have you done this?

After the questions, explain the real meanings of their answers, and thank them for being such great sports.

Choose your participants carefully. They should be guys who are not easily embarrassed and who are somewhat outgoing. Be sure to use this game to affirm them for being good sports. The goal of *Happy Hobbies* is to have fun and to focus on what people are like.

Who Are You? (5 minutes)

Distribute paper and pencils. Say something like: **Who are you? Right away, of course, you will think of your name as the correct answer to my question. Instead, I want you to describe yourself without using your name. Write down as much as you can in the next two minutes.**

After the two minutes are up, ask for a few of them to share *some* of what they wrote on their papers. When a person states a physical characteristic, ask how many others described themselves "physically" (such as blond hair, tall, ugly, dark-skinned, etc.). When someone relates a social characteristic, ask how many others also described themselves in "social" terms (such as Mr. and Mrs. Jones' daughter, Eileen's boyfriend, a good friend). Do the same for "mental" (a good Christian, a Lutheran, a witness), or another general category (such as emotional or vocational). The idea is to see *how* they describe themselves.

Stress that these papers are personal and secret—no one else will see them. Then you can encourage them to be very honest in their answers.

Discussion (7 minutes)

Next, focus the questions on *where* they get their self-concepts. Ask: **How did you learn those ideas about yourself?** (From other people, experiences, introspection, etc.) **Which people are most influential in forming your identity?** (Parents, best friends, teachers, coaches, etc.) Discuss how identities are formed.

Ask: **Are these descriptions of yourselves true—that is, do they correspond with reality? How do you know?** (They may or may not be true—often, however, our ideas about ourselves are false because they are based on false information or ideals.) **How does your self-concept affect your performance?** (It can hold you back, push you forward, or make you complacent and satisfied.)

This is an important discussion, so make sure they take it seriously. Possible answers are in parentheses.

Hey Simpson (5 minutes)

Say something like: **There was a song making the rounds a few years ago that has quite a bit of meaning. Instead of singing it tonight, I want you to listen to the words as I read. It's called, ''Hey Simpson''.**

1. When I was just eleven
   We had a fat boy on our block;
   His name was Leonard Simpson
   And we laughed at him a lot.

   Hey Simpson—fatty, fatty, two-by-four,
   Saw you hug the ugly girl next door.

2. Simpson wore bib overalls
   His old man cut his hair;
   He wore old army high-top boots
   and sleeveless underwear.
   We played a joke on him one day
   We let him join our club.
   We carved his name upon the door
   And splattered it with mud.
   We stood him up in front of us
   And this is what we sang:

   Hey Simpson—fatty, fatty, two-by-four,
   Saw you hug the ugly girl next door.

3. [Optional verse]
   Ole Simpson had a girlfriend,
   She wasn't any rose;
   She had long flowing black hair
   That came out through her nose,
   She wore ''Coke-bottle'' glasses
   Over her crossed eyes.
   She was pigeon-toed with legs that bo▸
   She really took the prize.

   Hey Simpson—fatty, fatty, two-by-four,
   Saw you hug the ugly girl next door.

4. That was eighteen years ago
   And now I'm twenty-nine;
   Simpson died some time ago
   A hero of some kind.
   They say a small young Jewish boy
   Was pestered by a gang;
   Simpson helped him get away,
   But was beat to death by chains.

   Hey Simpson—fatty, fatty, two-by-four
   Saw you hug the ugly girl next door.

As you discuss the song ask: **How did you feel when you heard the last chorus? Why?** (Most probably felt sorry for Simpson, or ashamed for the narrator. Some may even feel guilty for laughing.) **Have you ever known someone like Simpson?** (Be ready to share about people you've known who were rejected by the world at large.) **Do you ever feel like him? When?** (Everyone has experienced a time when he or she just didn't fit in or was unappreciated.)

Talk-to (3 minutes)

Say something like: **Strange, isn't it, as you think of poor, fat Leonard Simpson, how his life nevertheless had meaning? He really was somebody special. His life counted for something, because he sacrificed himself for someone else.**

It's strange how sometimes people you never thought would make it . . . make it. (Give examples of someone from your high school experience who surprised people by succeeding in some way.)

There was once a guy who, at the age of seven, thought you could hatch an egg by sitting on it yourself. He actually tried it. He was kicked out of school after only three months because he supposedly didn't have the ability to learn. He was especially bad at math. As a teenager he got a job selling newspapers and candy on the commuter train, and one day, the train had already started to roll when he came running alongside. A brakeman reached out, squeezed the kid's head between both hands and hoisted him onto the train. Before long, the boy started losing his hearing.

By the way, that guy's name was Thomas Edison. Just another person who some people thought would never make it, but who made it.

Each of us has the potential to become the person we really want to be. I think there are three factors that keep people from realizing that potential.

The first is a weak outlook. They say "Things would be different if my parents weren't like they are, or if my school wasn't like it is, or if the world wasn't like it is," and so on. The second factor that gets in the way is a weak faith. What do you really believe about yourself, about other people, about God? Faith is expecting something to really happen, or to be a reality, not just an illusion. Finally, some people suffer from a weak love. They say, "I love you if." "If you send me a Christmas card, I'll send you a Christmas card." Or "I love you because." "Because you're nice to me, or because you're beautiful, I'll love you." Strong love, however, says, "I love you regardless." "Regardless of how you look, how stubborn, or how resentful you are, I'll love you." This is love in its purest form—unconditional love. And it is the kind of love God has for you."

WORKOUT

Bible Search (15 minutes)

Distribute the worksheets, New Testaments, and pencils. Then have group members write on the backs of their sheets their ideas of God's view of them. After a minute or two, have them turn over their sheets and answer the questions. Here is the worksheet. (Possible answers are in parentheses.)

1. The Bible is God's letter to us. What do you think it means when someone writes to us? What do you think it means that God has written to us? What does that say about us? (If God thought enough of us to send us a letter, we must be pretty special to Him.)

2. Look at 1 John 4:7-12. What does this passage teach us about ourselves? (We are very valuable to God—He loved us enough to send Jesus to die for us.)

a. vv. 7-8 (God is love.)   d. v. 11 (We should love others.)
b. v. 9 (God showed His love.)   e. v. 12 (God can live in us.)
c. v. 10 (God sent His Son to die for our sins.)

3. Notice the changes in God's concept of us in Romans 5:6-11.

a. v. 6 (We were ungodly.)   d. vv. 9-10 (Saved from wrath)
b. vv. 7-8 (While we were sinners   e. v. 11 (Reconciliation)
     Christ died for us.)
c. v. 9 (Just think of what He will do for us!)

4. Being a member of God's family suggests some ways we should look at ourselves and others. What does Galatians 3:26-29 teach us?

a. v. 26 (We are His sons.)   c. v. 29 (We are His heirs.)
b. v. 28 (We are united in Christ.)

When you reprint this make sure you leave room for answers.

During their work, make sure that everyone is answering all the questions. Be available to trouble-shoot.

5. What does John 15:14-15 say about our relationship with God? (He calls us "friends."—We are chosen people.)

6. As God's friends and sons, we belong to Christ's body. Look at 1 Corinthians 12:4-30 to see what that means.

a. vv. 4-6 (We have gifts.)
b. v. 7 (We have the Spirit.)
c. vv. 12-13 (We are in the Body.)

d. vv. 14-16, 21-24 (Each of us has a unique role to play.)
e. vv. 17-20 (Each role is valuable.)
f. What is your gift?

WRAP-UP

I Am Somebody! (5 minutes)

After the *Bible Search,* say something like: **I hope you got the very personal message from those verses—you are very special to God. And His opinion of you counts more than that of anyone else on earth. In fact, knowing that you are loved by God should free you to really know and feel that you are** *somebody.* **Right now I am going to read a series of statements, descriptions of people. After each one, I want the whole group to repeat in unison, "I am somebody."**

Though I'm really straight and wear red argyle sox and have pimples and people call me a "nerd" . . . (I am somebody.)

Though I'm a football player, and you only like me when I win, and you snarl at me when I fumble . . . (I am somebody.)

Though I'm a policeman, and a lot of people hate my guts and call me a pig . . . (I am somebody.)

Though I'm a school teacher, and you don't like the rules I must try to enforce . . . (I am somebody.)

Though I'm from the Midwest and live on a farm and work side by side with my dad every night after school . . . (I am somebody.)

Though I am old, and no one listens to me any more or even wants to come and see me . . . (I am somebody.)

Though I am not the most popular girl on campus and have never held any offices or made any outstanding achievements . . . (I am somebody.)

Are you somebody? A lot of us are not sure. You can begin to strengthen your outlook, your faith, and your love by accepting yourself as the unique and loved creation of God. God made you . . . think of that! And He wants to use you, just as you are. If He loves you, can you love yourself? Are you willing to be used by Him?

In the left margin:

If you have time, take a few minutes to discuss their answers.

As always, the leader's enthusiasm is the key to the success of this activity.

Psalm 139 (3 minutes)

Distribute copies of Psalm 139 omitting verses 19-22. Read the chapter together, out loud. Encourage them to read this psalm each night before going to bed, for the next week. Close in prayer.

Use *The Living Bible* for readability.

Options for Further Study

These films are excellent discussion starters for a session on identity or self-worth.

Claude (3 minutes)
Claude is a small, animated boy living in an opulent house and belonging to conformist, cliché-ridden parents. "Claude, can't you do anything right?", says Mother; "You'll never amount to anything, Claude," says Father. But Claude ignores them both, having better things to do with a small black box, and finally takes revenge in a surprise ending. *Claude* is available through San Antonio Youth for Christ, 306 West Mistletoe, San Antonio, Texas, 78212, (512) 736-4406.

Eagle Beak (10 minutes)
This film focuses on a high school girl and her feelings about herself. She would like to be like the ceramic ballerina sitting on her dresser, but she feels like an ugly misfit. The focus on her feelings is her nose and her schoolmates' comments about it. *Eagle Beak* is available from Y.F.C. of Greater Houston, Mars Hill/Campus Life Productions, 9302 Wilcrest, Houston, Texas, 77099, (713) 879-9800.

Additional Resources

Sometimes I Feel Like a Nobody (Tim Stafford, Tyndale House)
This is a very practical book for young people, centering on "self-concept." if possible, make it available for purchase or loan by your students.

Campus Life Guide for Student Leadership (Youth for Christ/U.S.A.)
This is a workbook for students—ideal for individual or small group use. It is available from Youth For Christ, Box 419, Wheaton, IL 60189, (312) 668-6600.

Nobody Like Me (Stan Campbell, Victor Books)
This twelve-week study of self-image is written for young teens, with a complete leader's book available. It focuses on the issues of failure, image-distorters, and popularity.

SESSION 6

THE POSSIBLE DREAM

WHERE CAN I TURN IN MY DESPAIR?

KEY CONCEPT	In a world threatened by nuclear holocaust and in a private world of shattered ideals and dreams, young people can feel overwhelming despair.
GOAL	This session will help young people discover the reality of true, lasting hope in Jesus Christ—for the world and for the individual.
OVERVIEW	Young people can feel overwhelmed by the problems of the world. Each day's headlines scream of terrorism, abortion, nuclear blackmail, racial violence, assasinations, famine, and other terrible global struggles. At the same time they may be faced with their own sets of personal conflicts, school failures, romance breakups, family disintegrations, etc. An understandable response to any one or a combination of these problems would be despair. But Christians have hope! The truth is that God is sovereign, and He loves us. And we can never be lost to His love. This session, therefore, will focus on the hope that is ours in Christ and will challenge young people to turn to Him in the midst of their struggles and to look beyond their present situations to their loving Heavenly Father. As you go through this session, remind your students to keep their eyes on Christ.
TIME REQUIRED	30-45 minutes
MATERIALS CHECKLIST	Materials needed for basic session: _____ Newspapers, poster board, and tape (*In the News*) _____ "Situation sheets" for discussion groups _____ New Testaments or Scripture sheets for Bible study _____ Pencils or pens _____ 3" x 5" cards for comments and counseling for *Close* Materials needed for optional activities: _____ Lemons for *Lemon Pass* _____ Situations, "grab bag" and paper (*World Poem*) _____ Projector, etc. for optional movies _____ Songs for optional "hunger songs" discussion
JUNIOR HIGH ADAPTATION	To make this session most effective with young teens, use the following: *Lemon Pass* (don't use *World Poem*); *In the News*; discussion as a whole group with a few junior high situations; Bible study; prayer circles; and *Close*.

WARM-UP

Optional Openers

Lemon Pass (7 minutes)

Divide into teams and seat them in parallel, single file lines. Have group members remove their shoes, and give each team a lemon. This is a race to see which team can pass the lemon from person to person, using only their feet to hold and pass the lemons. The first team to pass the lemon the entire length of the team (or down and back if there aren't very many team members), wins.

The goal of this game is to have fun. It also is a picture of the truth that "sometimes life hands you a lemon." If they aren't too damaged, turn the lemons into lemonade for your refreshments.

World Poem (8 minutes)

Before the meeting, prepare slips of paper with pressing world problems written on them (one on each). Place them into a paper bag. Now, divide the group into smaller units—these can be couples or "teams," and the units do not all have to be the same size. Give each a piece of paper and a pencil. Explain that one person from each unit will draw a "world problem" from the bag. Their job is to write a poem about that particular problem. Give them four or five minutes to write, and then have them read their poems. Some of the world problems could include: hunger, racism, nuclear armament, civil war, terrorism, pollution, abortion, totalitariansim, poverty, earthquakes, violence, and others.

This is meant to be serious, so introduce it as such. Even so, you will have some humorous poems. Read them anyway. Your students may protest that they can't write, but encourage them to try. You, and they, will be surprised at the good results. Obviously, the goal of this activity is to begin thinking about world problems.

In the News (8 minutes)

Mount two or three poster boards on the front wall. Then, distribute newspapers throughout the whole group. Ask group members to scan the papers and tear out stories about terrible problems in the world, anything from highjackings, terrorism, and war, to hunger, poverty, and crime. Then they should bring the articles to the front and tape them to the poster boards. After the boards are full, summarize the stories for the group. Then ask: **Is this an accurate picture of our world today?** (Some may feel it is accurate; others may believe it reflects media exaggeration of problems.) **How does it make you feel?** (Some may admit to feeling helpless, anxious or even angry about the world's troubles.) **When have you personally really felt despair—as though everything was hopeless?** (Discuss answers.) **Is there, as Sartre put it, "no exit"—no way out?**

Newsprint will dirty their hands, so have washcloths available. Also, be sure to pass around a garbage bag for the leftover papers. Any part of the paper is fair game, even the entertainment, sports, and comics sections.

Don't spend too long on your summary—this activity is designed as an "opener," not the "meat."

Talk-to (3 minutes)

Say something like: **One man entered history, not by accident, but by voluntary choice. That man entered from outside the room—something no one else ever did. He was a carpenter, and He made a door in the room of our hopelessness. He said, 'I am the door. If anyone exits after Me, he will get out.' Having made the door, He Himself went out of the room and made a way for us. He is the way, the truth, the life . . . the exit!**

What Jesus, the carpenter, says is this: through Him you can enter a new life, abundant and full. It is easy to feel despair when you read the headlines, become aware of the condition of the world, and, at the same time, are critically aware of your own inner conflicts. But Jesus said, "Here on earth you will have many trials and sorrows; but cheer up, for I have overcome the world" (John 16:33, TLB). With His new light, we get a new task in life. It becomes our responsibility to make the world a better place, and we have the power to actually make a difference.

This is an important transition from the global to personal problems. Be sure to emphasize the reality of Christ.

And if I know Christ, I can be assured that He knows what I am going through. He has suffered for me. I can also know that Christ is the goal of history. He will come again. He thus gives us a new outlook on the future. Everything is now different. There is no longer a misty, sinister landscape. And, if the last hour belongs to us, we do not need to fear the next minute.

WORKOUT

Discussion (10 minutes)

Introduce the discussion by saying something like: **Let's bring our thoughts away from the world in general and talk about our despair. How does Jesus relate to that?**

Divide the crowd into three groups and give everyone a discussion sheet with three situations on it. (Each group will have different situations.) They should discuss their three situations one at a time and answer two questions about each: (1) Would you have a feeling of hopelessness and why?; (2) What would Jesus' answer be? They should give Bible references to back up their answers if possible. Here are the discussion sheets.

Group Number One

1. You are a senior and have just learned that you flunked a final exam. You won't be able to graduate.
2. You have just learned that you have an illness that will hospitalize you for three months.
3. Your parents, whom you love, are getting a divorce.

Group Number Two

1. Your father has lost his job and so your family has to move to another state. You've lived in that house all your life.
2. You're a new Christian, and your parents strongly oppose your faith. They've just said, "No more church, no more youth group."
3. You recently got your driver's license and have just sideswiped a parked car.

Group Number Three

1. Your girlfriend (or boyfriend), for whom you really care, has just broken up with you for someone else.
2. You're the only Christian in a class of cynics, and they've just cut you down for the tenth time.
3. Your father just had a heart attack and is not expected to live.

After five or six minutes, have the groups report. Listen to the reports carefully, noting especially their comments on how Christ could help. Your will probably hear two types of despair: grief and/or shame over the present, and fear and uncertainty of the future. Summarize and comment where appropriate, and move on to the Bible study.

Bible Study (7 minutes)

Read Romans 8: 1, 17-22, 24-25, 28-39 while everyone follows along. Then discuss, as a whole group, the question: **What is the Christian's hope?**

Remember, it takes time to break into and out of groups, so form them right where they are sitting.

Each discussion sheet will only have *three* situations listed, and each student should have a sheet. At the bottom of the sheets, be sure to write the two questions to be answered about each situation.

It may be easier to photocopy these verses or to read the entire chapter.

You should hear these answers:
- No future condemnation (vv. 1, 34)
- Future glory (vv. 17-18, 30)
- God's plan is working in our lives (v. 28)
- The opposition is beaten (v. 31)
- We have right standing with God (v. 33)
- Jesus is pleading our case (v. 34)
- Nothing can block God's love (vv. 35-39)

Be sure to make applications of these facts to the previous real-life situations.

WRAP-UP

Challenge (2 minutes)

Reiterate the main truths emphasized in the session. They are:
1. God is in control of the world.
2. What we see around us is not the *whole* story—eternity waits.
3. God loves us individually, in the middle of our problems.
4. Real hope is ours through Christ.
5. No matter what we are facing or where we are, we can never be lost to God's love.
6. We can overcome whatever we have to face through Christ's strength.
7. We should bring hope to the world, telling people about Christ and working for peace and justice.

Prayer (5 minutes)

Using the groups from the *Discussion*, have them get into three circles and pray together. They should pray around the circle with everyone praying a sentence. The first time around, encourage them to thank God for the hope Christ has given. The second time around, they should pray for friends who are still "without hope."

Close (2 minutes)

Because this session touches on some very personal areas, this would be a good time to encourage group members to seek counseling if they are really struggling. Distribute 3" x 5" cards and have everyone write a sentence evaluation of the session. Those who want to get together with you to talk should add their names and phone numbers. Collect all the cards. Encourage group members to memorize Romans 8:35-39 during the week.

Option for Further Study

Play "We are the World," "Do They Know It's Christmas," "Tears are Not Enough," and other "hunger" songs, and discuss them in the light of world needs and Christians' responses.

Additional Resource

The Campus Life Guide to Surviving High School (Verne Becker, Tyndale House) This very practical volume is written for students to help them through personal and spiritual struggles faced in high school.

These are not your "sermon" notes for a wrap-up. Your job is to encourage the students to discover these truths for themselves. Put these in the back of your mind so that you'll recognize them when they come up in the discussion.

Often young people will avoid praying in a group because it is threatening. Don't let them discuss; encourage everyone to participate.

SESSION 7

WHAT'S THE DIFFERENCE?

WHAT DIFFERENCE DOES CHRIST MAKE IN DAILY LIFE?

KEY CONCEPT

Young Christians, in their idealism, can be surprised and even feel overwhelmed by the normal everyday strains, pressures, and conflicts of life.

GOAL

This session asks young people to consider the *true* difference that being a Christian makes in life's daily occurrences.

OVERVIEW

Because of youthful idealism, the glowing testimonies heard, and even some sermons stressing "Christian success," many young people have the idea that the Christian life should be conflict and problem free. Then, when they face problems, they are confused and don't know what to do. To make matters worse, often it seems as though things go better for non-Christians. This gap between idealism and reality leads to discouragement and frustration, and it may cause them to miss the real meaning of living with and for Christ. This session, therefore, will focus on the difference that Christ can make in their lives. As you go through this session, be sure to paint a realistic view of the world, identifying the real feelings of group members. Then, challenge them to keep their personal focus on Christ, not on others or their circumstances.

TIME REQUIRED

30-45 minutes

MATERIALS CHECKLIST

Materials needed for basic session:
____ Two people to act in the role play
____ Pencils
____ *Stress and Strain Gain* charts
____ Bibles
____ Worksheets (*Bible Search*)
____ Poster board and marker or chalkboard and chalk
____ Cards (*Action Plan*)

Materials needed for optional activities:
____ Hats, music, and prize (*Musical Hats*)

JUNIOR HIGH ADAPTATION

Junior highers need to understand that Christ is with us in the middle of our problems; He doesn't eliminate all of them. Therefore, this session will be very appropriate for young teens. All of the "categories" in the *Stress and Strain Gain* chart apply to their lives. Just be sure, however, to give them specific examples with which they can identify.

WARM-UP

Optional Opener

Musical Hats (5-8 minutes)

This can be done with the whole group or with a small, representative number. Give each person a hat and have everyone stand in a circle with all but one wearing a hat. When the music starts, each person must take the hat off the person in front and place it on his or her own head. This should continue until the music stops. When the music stops, the person without a hat must sit down. Remove another hat and repeat the process. Continue the game until a winner is determined.

With a large group, use some of the hats worn to the meeting. Also, you may want to divide into smaller circles which compete simultaneously. The goal of this activity is to have fun and to illustrate how we often feel we're "wearing many hats."

Role Play (5 minutes)

Begin this by saying something like: **In talking with many of you, I sense that you are really concerned that your lives reflect the difference that only Christ can make. And yet, in the everyday occurrences of life, things happen to us just like they seem to happen to non-Christians. And, for some of us, it seems like we get all the bad breaks while the non-Christian has everything going for him. This apparent inconsistency bothers some of us as we think about the influence we want to have at school. To help us "feel" with what I've been talking about, two volunteers are going to role play a typical situation.**

Using two adult leaders—or volunteer group members—improvise a role play that will illustrate a Christian boy who can't seem to get things going for himself. He is conversing with a non-Christian friend who is finding success in everything—girls, grades, sports, etc. The Christian wants to involve the non-Christian in the youth group, but the friend responds, "Why should I get involved in this Christian thing? It doesn't do you any good."

Choose your "actors" carefully and talk to them before the meeting about their roles. Don't discuss this afterward. It is only meant to set the stage for the rest of the session.

WORKOUT

Stress and Strain Gain (5 minutes)

Say: **In just a minute, we're going to fill out *Stress and Strain Gain* charts. On it you'll find several typical areas of strain. It's designed to help determine if these stress points are common in the lives of most young people, if they affect the Christian particularly, and, most important, if they affect you. Honesty is the key, so fill them out carefully.**

Distribute the charts and pencils. (See sample chart on page 38)

Discussion (13 minutes)

Break the group into small groups to discuss the charts. Assign a discussion leader to each group.

The discussion can be guided by the leader choosing several of the problem descriptions at random (or one at a time), and asking the group, "How do non-Christian kids who have this problem try to handle it?" and "How do you think a Christian would do it differently?" He or she should lead toward the general question, "What difference then does it make to be a Christian?"

Allow time to break into groups.

The function of this discussion time is not to *answer* the question, "what's the difference?" but to intensify the awareness of the problem. The leader needs to be careful here not to intrude and bail out students, give them answers, or show too much agreement with those who have centered in on the real issues. The answers will come, but not necessarily at this point.

STRESS AND STRAIN GAIN							
STRESS FROM . . .	TRUE FOR MOST KIDS?		CHRISTIAN KIDS?		TRUE FOR ME?		
	YES	NO	YES	NO	YES	NO	
1. Conflicts with parents.	☐	☐	☐	☐	☐	☐	
2. Trying to be myself with others	☐	☐	☐	☐	☐	☐	
3. Temptations to do things I know aren't right	☐	☐	☐	☐	☐	☐	
4. Fear of what others think of me	☐	☐	☐	☐	☐	☐	
5. Being satisfied with myself	☐	☐	☐	☐	☐	☐	
6. Desires that seem wrong	☐	☐	☐	☐	☐	☐	
7. Uncertain about my relationship with God	☐	☐	☐	☐	☐	☐	
8. Conflicts with teachers and other school officials	☐	☐	☐	☐	☐	☐	
9. Awkwardness in new situations with new people	☐	☐	☐	☐	☐	☐	
10. Acting badly or out of turn	☐	☐	☐	☐	☐	☐	

Reproduce this chart. Add other stressful situations specific for your young people.

Bible Search (10 minutes)

Say something like: **By now you have probably discovered that being a Christian doesn't automatically remove all of a person's problems. It's frustrating, though, when our everyday experience often doesn't confirm the difference that we expect Christ to make in our lives. And that brings us down to the basic question: "What is the difference that Christ really makes in our lives?" Here is a worksheet with some Bible verses on it. Read each verse and write down what it says about the difference Christ makes in our lives.** Distribute the worksheets with these verses on them. The answers are in parentheses. Discuss when finished

Add other verses.

Joshua 1:9—(God is with us no matter what we face.)
Psalm 10:16-18—(God hears us and encourages us.)
Psalm 32:1-7—(God forgives our sins and surrounds us with His unfailing love.)
Psalm 71:20-21—(God will restore us and honor us.)
Romans 8:28—(God is working all things for good.)
Romans 8:29—(God is making us like Christ.)
Romans 8:38-39—(We can never be lost to God's love.)

WRAP-UP

Talk-to (7 minutes)

You might want to make a flip chart listing the principles and how they make a "difference" or simply list them as you go on a chalkboard.

Say something like: **At this point, I'd like to share with you three basic principles that have helped me understand how Christ works in my life to make a difference:**

1. *The Christian accepts him or herself for what he or she is, a sinner.* The Christian is free to recognize the fact that he does need help. He doesn't expect to be able to straighten out his own life and solve all his problems himself, and he knows that God doesn't expect him to be perfect either. Knowing we are sinners means that we don't have to pretend about our failings or our problems. This doesn't mean we like them or enjoy blowing it, but it does mean we never have to pretend to ourselves or to others about being something we're not (Romans 7).

2. *The Christian realizes that God loves him or her anyway.* Often in relationships with others we get the impression that we have to do things to be loved. But God doesn't base His relationship with us on performance. He accepts us because He loves us, knowing perfectly well what we are like. Romans 5:6 gives us Paul's perspective on this concept. Another good illustration is in the story of the Prodigal Son.

3. *The Christian receives power from Christ to be different.* This principle reflects Galatians 2:20 and the "Christ in you" concept that makes Christianity unique. In addition to this verse, check out John 15 where Jesus talks about the Vine and the branches.

Together, these principles sketch the following "difference that it makes for Christians" when we discover problems and pressures in our lives:

• We always have the assurance that we are worthwhile persons because our value isn't something "earned" by doing good.

• We always have the confidence that God loves us—no matter what (and we can never lose that love).

• We always have Christ to rely on for the power to become different and better persons—to do what's right and best.

Action Plan (5 minutes)

Distribute cards and instruct group members to choose one "conflict" area in which they have recently struggled. They should write that area on the top of the card. Underneath it, they should write, "Pray about." Tell them to fill in that blank. In other words, write what should they talk to God about relative to that specific problem.

It would help to have these cards printed ahead of time.

Next, have them write the phrase, "Attitude changes" and tell them to follow it with the changes in their attitudes that should be made in light of the principles that you gave in your *Talk-to*. Finally, they should write, "Steps to take." After this they should write two or three specific actions that they will take to resolve the conflict or correct the problem. Encourage group members to keep these cards in their Bibles and to refer to them during their quiet times. Close in prayer.

Option for Further Study

Campus Life magazine features true stories each month of how Christian high school students apply their faith to specific challenges in their lives. Choose a couple of these and make copies for everyone—discuss how their situations are similar.

Additional Resource

Faith Workout (Bill Myers, Victor Books)
This lively study of the Book of James works through the difference Christ makes in the nitty-gritty areas of life.

MAKING CHRIST LORD   ROMANS 6:11-19

SESSION 8

GOD! AND HOW?

HOW CAN I PUT GOD IN THE CENTER OF MY LIFE?

KEY CONCEPT

Christian young people tend to make idealistic, "dedication" decisions which last for a short period of time instead of learning how to live for Christ on a daily basis.

GOAL

This session will help young people understand what it means to make Christ Lord of one's life.

OVERVIEW

By the time a Christian young person nears the end of his or her high school experience, he or she has probably been exposed to scores of high-powered, persuasive, sermonic challenges. In response, decisions are made to "be a better Christian" by doing something (such as have a "quiet time," love people, witness daily, pray, etc.). These dedication decisions, however, are usually short-lived with the person falling back into the familiar routine. After awhile, these young people begin to feel a sort of "conviction fatigue," and they wonder if the Christian life really works. In contrast, the lordship of Christ is not a one-time, lifetime decision. Instead, it is a day-by-day process of yielding our lives of His control. This session will emphasize this truth and will challenge young people to put it into practice in their lives. This session will stand on its own but would fit best following session 3, "All of Me."

TIME REQUIRED

30-45 minutes

MATERIALS CHECKLIST

Material needed for basic session:
____ Worksheets (*Do It Now!*)
____ Pencils
____ New Testaments or copies of Romans 6:11-19
____ *How a Christian Grows* worksheets
____ Chalkboard and chalk, or poster board and felt-tip marker

Materials need for optional activities:
____ Cards (*Instant Drama*)
____ Worksheets (*Dedication*)

JUNIOR HIGH ADAPTATION

It is never too early to understand the lordship of Christ; therefore, junior high would be an ideal time for this session. The *Warm-up* activities may be used as they are with only a few minor changes to the *Do It Now* worksheet (for instance, ask for a different number instead of "Social Security"). When you go through the lordship of Christ diagram, be sure to use terms and examples that they can understand. You don't want this session to be too "conceptual."

WARM-UP

Optional Opener

Instant Drama (10 minutes)

Break the crowd into small groups. Have the groups send representatives to the front to draw a card on which has been written an item which they as a group must act out. Give them about five minutes to prepare, and then have them demonstrate, one group at a time. Possible items could include: Food—stuffed pepper, enchilada, Denver omelet, coffee perking, pizza, banana split, bacon and eggs cooking; machines—typewriter, vacuum cleaner, hedge-trimmer, lawnmower, egg beater, computer, car jack.

The purpose of this is to have fun and to work together on a project.

Do It Now! (5 minutes)

Give everyone the following worksheet and a pencil and tell them to work independently and to do what the paper says. The goal is to finish first.

Convey the sense of urgency to this activity—that they should finish it as soon as possible. The purpose is to have fun and to illustrate what it means to follow instructions carefully.

DO IT NOW!

Do what the instructions say. Do not talk to anyone else. If you have a question, raise your hand for assistance.

Read all the instructions before proceeding.

1. Write your name on the back of the paper.

2. Count the number of lights in the room and write that number here.

3. Write your Social Security number here: _____ - _____ - _____ .

4. When you get this far, stand up immediately and shout, "Ah ha!"

5. Do one push-up.

6. Write your first name backward: _____ .

7. Ask a staff person for the time and write it here: _____ .

8. Take off one shoe.

9. Write three words formed from the letters in CAMPAIGN: _____ , _____ , and _____ .

10. Turn to the person on your right and give your biggest smile.

11. Turn around rapidly in a circle three times.

12. Circle every number on this sheet.

13. Doodle quickly in this space:

14. Rip the paper in half.

15. Disregard insructions 1-14.

16. Sit quietly and watch everyone else.

When everyone has settled down, ask what kind of point that exercise makes about following instructions. Mention that by following God's directions we can often avoid "going around in cirlces" and being detoured by foolish action.

Introduction (5 minutes)

Say something like: **You and I are pretty complex. We are each a unique combination of the physical, social, mental, and spiritual. As we take honest looks at our lives, however, we would have to admit that some areas are not God's property. What do you think you could do to make a change?** (Discuss briefly.)

Have them just give examples quickly. Don't spend much time on this.

Some of you, if you have been Christians for awhile, may have heard a lot of the following words: dedication, yielding, surrender, full commitment, consecration, rededication, sanctification. How do you make these things actually work in your life? (Pause for answers. If a few suggestions are offered, fine; but don't discuss this long.)

Some of us have gotten all psyched up at a camp or in a special meeting and have made some kind of "dedication decision" or whatever, only to fall on our noses before the week was out. In fact the longest most of these kind of decisions seem to last in about two weeks. Why? (Discuss briefly.)

Wills (5 minutes)

Say: **Everybody stand up and hold your right hand up in the air. Now, take your right hand and pull on your left ear. Now, use your right hand to pat yourself on the head. Pat your stomach. OK, you can sit down.**

This can also be done very effectively with one or two individuals who stand in front of the whole group.

Before you decide that I've just cracked up, let me ask you a question: whose will controlled your right hand? (Accept all suggestions.)

Some of you say you did it, but you never would have done all those things without me being here. Some of you say it was my will. Well then, if I'm so powerful, let me try again: we'll take out the bulb from this lamp here, and everybody come up and put your finger in the socket. (Prepare the lamp.) Why aren't you coming? (Don't let anyone take you up on your suggestion!)

The point is this: you don't do everything I tell you to do, but you did let me control your right hand a minute ago. You chose to cooperate with me. In other words, it was a *combination of two wills*—yours and mine. You let me carry out my will, but it was your hand doing the patting!

WORKOUT

Bible Discussion (7 minutes)

Introduce this by saying something like: **Well that's the way it works with God. You can decide that He knows better and begin to allow His will to control yours. You march into those problem areas and you admit that you will only gets you into more trouble—so you agree to cooperate with His will.**

Have everyone open to Romans 6:11-19 and read the passage silently. Afterward ask: **What seems to be the only thing you can do to bring about improvement in some area of your life?** (Discuss)

Have them read the passage again, this time inserting one of their problem areas every time they see the words "sin" or "wickedness." For example if "overeating" is something a person can't control, he could read, "Do not let overeating reign in your mortal body so that you obey its evil desires" (v. 12). (Allow time for rereading.)

Talk-to and Worksheets (15 minutes)

Say something like: **I can read most of your minds right now; you're saying to yourselves,** *Sounds great—but how do I do it?* **That's what I want to explain for the next few minutes. Here's a fill-in-the-blank sheet called** *How a Christian Grows* **for you to use as we go along.**

(This sheet is printed at the end of the session.)

The person who initiates growth, who gets us moving off dead center is God. Fill in blank at #1.

We have to understand that He is more interested in our growing and maturing than we could ever be. He sees all kinds of potential in us, and He wants to bring it out. Listen to some of these Scriptures. (Read, or have young people read as many as you have time for.)

The cycle begins when you and I finally decide to let Him do His thing. Fill in "I" in blank at #2.

We turn over the control of various areas of our intellects, attitudes, values, emotions, relationships, thoughts, habits, motives, desires—as much as we can—to the one we have acknowledged as Lord. We've already read the passage from Romans 6; some others are . . . (Read Scriptures from sheet.)

This yielding permits Christ to become Lord of these areas. Write the word "permits" along the arrow toward #3.

Do you know what a "lord" is? British young people would be more familiar with the term than we are, since they live around nobility called lords, and the upper house of their Parliament is the House of Lords. But all of us at least know what a landlord is; he's the person who owns the building, controls what goes on inside, has the power to kick out whoever he doesn't like, etc. Why? Because it's his house! He's the boss. Well, that's sort of what happens when we permit Christ to be Lord of more and more of our lives. We give Him the right to control what goes on. There's a difference, of course, in that He is no brute or selfish moneygrubber; He guides and leads us through the power of His own example as explained in the Bible. Read verses.

We can "give God permission" because He does not force Himself on us. He allows us to exercise our wills.

As we keep yielding various areas to the lordship of Christ, He eventually comes to control more and more of our "house." We are on a continuum from zero percent Christ-control to 100-percent Christ-control. Only you can say at what point you are on the continuum: 40 percent? 75 percent? 20 percent? Which way is the present trend—toward more and more lordship for Christ, or less and less?

Draw the same thing on a chalkboard or poster board as you talk.

One of the major things He does, once He's allowed to be Lord, is to release the power of the *Holy Spirit.* (Fill in those two words at #4.)

Ephesians 3:16 talks about strengthening "with power through His Spirit in your inner being." When the Holy Spirit's power is released in your life, He produces all sorts of by-products." (Write "produces" along the arrow toward #5 and fill in the blank with the word "sin.")

One of these by-products is "sensitivity to sin." Listen to this passage from Galatians 5:16-21. (Read the passage.)

The unleashed Holy Spirit also produces other things such as the power to acknowledge Christ as Lord, the power to witness, improvements in our characters, and the feeling of being loved. Now that the Holy Spirit has pointed out some problems in our lives—what are we going to do about it? We can stifle, squelch, or ignore Him. But this will put us on a dead-end street toward guilt, rebellion, and the lack of power as well as the lack of feeling of being loved that we have enjoyed.

Or we can face up to this new problem which the Holy Spirit has illuminated, which requires that we yield and confess once again regarding this new area. (Write the word "requires" along the arrow pointing back toward 2.) Maybe we didn't really know it was there before—but now we do, and we're faced with the familiar question: will we allow Christ to be Lord of this new area or not? As this cycle goes on and on, we keep growing and increasing the percentage of Christ-controlled living.

Each day, your life and mine get bigger and bigger. We have concerns and problems now that we never dreamed of two years ago. The physical, mental, social, and religious parts of us keep unfolding with new dilemmas. And this is why we must keep growing, turning over these new areas to Christ's control, which will release the Holy Spirit to help us deal with them and point up even further adjustments that need to be made.

Feedback (2 minutes)

Ask for questions about what you just presented and clarify what they may have missed or misunderstood.

WRAP-UP

Challenge (3 minutes)

Explain that you hope this discussion brings the vague ideas of "dedication" or "doing better" down out of the clouds. Point out that the problem with so many of our "decisions" in the past is that they've been too general; we've given "our whole lives" to Christ's control without breaking them down into bite-size pieces. Hence, in attempting to give everything, we actually gave nothing.

Encourage group members to give God a starting point. Tell them to make sure that what they select is something important, something they really need help on. Ask that each one yield that area to Christ's control.

Say: **I can tell you right now that if you try to make this work under your own steam, you'll fail. You may think you can crank up these products of the Holy Spirit's power through your own power instead, but you'll soon find out differently. You'll short-circuit the whole cycle. The beautiful part is**

Give an anonymous example of somebody who yielded something specific and saw results.

realizing that you are not alone; you do have a Lord, a "boss," who can bring about real change in your life. Let's get started!

Action (3 minutes)

Take a few minutes to let group members pray silently about what that first problem area will be. Then pray out loud for them.

Give them the assignment to take home the "Lordship of Christ" worksheet and read through all of the other scriptures during the next week.

Be sure to follow-through on this assignment at your next meeting.

HOW A CHRISTIAN GROWS

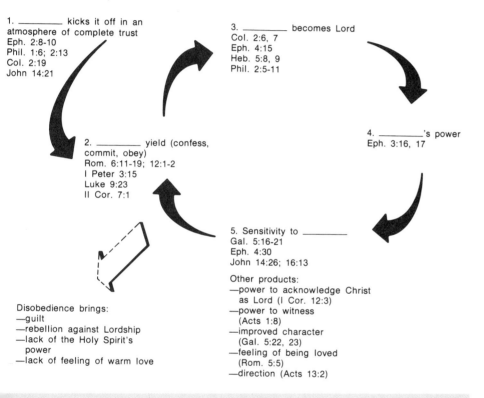

1. _____ kicks it off in an atmosphere of complete trust
Eph. 2:8-10
Phil. 1:6; 2:13
Col. 2:19
John 14:21

2. _____ yield (confess, commit, obey)
Rom. 6:11-19; 12:1-2
I Peter 3:15
Luke 9:23
II Cor. 7:1

3. _____ becomes Lord
Col. 2:6, 7
Eph. 4:15
Heb. 5:8, 9
Phil. 2:5-11

4. _____'s power
Eph. 3:16, 17

5. Sensitivity to _____
Gal. 5:16-21
Eph. 4:30
John 14:26; 16:13

Other products:
—power to acknowledge Christ as Lord (I Cor. 12:3)
—power to witness (Acts 1:8)
—improved character (Gal. 5:22, 23)
—feeling of being loved (Rom. 5:5)
—direction (Acts 13:2)

Disobedience brings:
—guilt
—rebellion against Lordship
—lack of the Holy Spirit's power
—lack of feeling of warm love

Option for Further Study

The attached worksheet entitled "God! And How?" would be an excellent base for a follow-up meeting. It explains to "environmental" Christians why their past efforts at growth may have failed. Distribute the worksheet blank except for titles and have the group work together in filling in the first column which describes the way things often are. Temporarily omit "control." Then go on to how things should be, again omitting "control." Then point out the crucial difference: in the first case the Christian is trying to muster up the by-products of yieldedness by sheer willpower. In the second, he admits that he can't do it alone and asks for Christ to take over.

Additional Resources

My Heart Christ's Home (Robert B. Munger, InterVarsity Press)
This little booklet pictures our lives as houses into which we invite Christ to live. Gradually, He wants to take over the whole house. It is very practical and would make an excellent handout.

Finding Faith (Andrew Knowles, A Lion Manual)
A colorful and practical guide to putting faith into practice in everyday life. Chapters
"The Heart of the Matter," "God's Chosen Rabble," and "Power for Life" would be
most applicable for this session.

GOD! AND HOW?

	The Typical Christian Life	What the Christian Life Should Be	Comment
Goal	Please God and do His service (or a specific service)	Glorify God by being conformed to the image of Christ	Examples: do God's will, witness, love, etc.
Means	Honest effort	I yield	"Honest effort" sounds good, but. . . .
Control	Self	Christ is Lord	Here's where the "typical" falls.
Power	Determination	Holy Spirit empowers	"Typical" = "grit teeth," "keep on keeping on". . . .
Attitude	Pride (when successful)	Humility	This pride splits more churches than doctrinal differences
Results	Frustration, discouragement	By-products and sensitivity to sin	Why these results in the "Typical"? Look at Control

SESSION 9

MINORITY TACTICS

HOW CAN I SHARE MY FAITH WITH MY FRIENDS?

KEY CONCEPT	Facing opposition to their faith, Christians will often be defensive and adopt a "survival" mentality.
GOAL	This session will challenge your young people to take the "offensive" in telling others about Christ.
OVERVIEW	Though Christian books and records are selling by the thousands, we live in a world that is not very sympathetic to Christians. In fact, the world's values are opposite Christ's, and true Christians are a distinct minority in society. Christian young people, especially those in public schools, know that this is true. Peers may laugh at their beliefs or greet them with profound indifference, and they are constantly pressured to do things that they know are wrong. In the face of this pressure, they may retreat to the safety of their Christian friends or take a defensive stance, hoping to protect themselves. Instead, however, Christians are called to act, to make a difference for Christ in their world. This session, therefore, will challenge students to use "minority tactics" to take the initiative and reach out to their friends and associates with love and with the Good News.
TIME REQUIRED	30-45 minutes
MATERIALS CHECKLIST	Materials needed for basic session: ____ Cards *(Real Life)* ____ New Testaments or copies of Philippians 1:12-30; 2:1-18 ____ Pencils/pens ____ Papers *(Battle Plan)* Materials needed for optional activities: ____ Items and bags *(Super Salesman)* ____ Prizes for *Super Salesman* ____ *Minority Tactics* worksheets
JUNIOR HIGH ADAPTATION	This is a relevant topic for junior highers. They need to be thinking about how to witness to their peers, and the session does not have to be changed very much. For *Real Life,* be sure to have an adult leader with each group and use situations with which they can identify. Also, do not use *Super Salesman* with your junior high group.

WARM-UP

Optional Opener

Super Salesman (8-10 minutes)

Encourage your ''salesman'' to be enthusiastic. The point of this game is to illustrate how difficult it is to ''sell'' something that we don't know much about (much like some people try to witness).

Choose three students and have them leave the room with an assistant who will give them their instructions. Bring them back into the room one at a time to give an imaginative and enthusiastic sales pitch for an item concealed in a brown paper bag. Give each one thirty seconds; they should *not* know what is in the bag. Then allow a short time for questions from the audience as to the usefulness and quality of the item. Of course the audience will know what is in each bag because you will reveal it to them just before the ''salesman'' enters the room. The items could include a wig, a can of deodorant, a bunch of grapes, a razor, etc. Award a prize to the best ''salesman.''

Don't give them time to prepare. It should be extemporaneous.

Real Life (10 minutes)

Divide into groups with about three or four students in each. Explain that one of their groups will have the opportunity to come forward and draw a ''real life situation'' out of a box and then act it out for the rest of the group. The situations could include: a few students making fun of another's Christian faith; students arguing with a Christian or two that Christian morality is out of date and old-fashioned; non-Christian adults explaining that education and knowledge are the answers to all of mankind's problems; a teacher or other person belittling the Bible, saying it is full of contradictions and a fairy tale; fellow workers pressuring a Christian to party with them after work; during lunch in the school cafeteria, popular students pressuring a Christian to give them the answers to the test.

Discussion (7 minutes)

Make the transition by saying something like: **Yes, it can be difficult to be a Christian in such a hostile environment. We are definitely in the minority! And when faced with such odds, it's easy to become discouraged or depressed or doubtful. But let me ask you this: instead of being completely overcome by all this opposition, both obvious and subtle, how can you as a Christian survive?**

Put yourself in this position: you have just spent a week at church camp, and it was great. God was real to you, and you decided that this year you were really going to live the Christian life. You return home to old friends, your family, your school, and suddenly you're hit with the hostility about which we've been talking; it's no longer ''in'' to be a Christian like at camp. What can you do to survive?

Let them discuss for awhile. They will respond with answers such as ''read the Bible,'' ''pray a lot,'' ''stick together as Christians,'' ''have more camp reunions,'' ''stay away from the old friends,'' ''read only Christian books,'' etc. Then hit them from the ''blind side'' with:

Wait a minute! We're making the same mistake that Christians have been making for hundreds of years! We're talking about ''survival'' and not about changing our world. Instead of wrapping a security blanket around ourselves, we need to be saying, ''How can we as Christians make a difference? How can we bring Christ to our hostile surroundings?'' We must take the offensive!

The early church in the first century faced unbelievable opposition. If you had been a Christian then, you would have been hunted down. Thousands of early believers were condemned and executed for their faith. They were a distinct minority, and yet they were on the offensive.

WORKOUT

Paul's Attitude (8 minutes)

Have everyone turn to Philippians 1:12-30, and give them time to read the entire passage. Then ask: **In what kind of situation is Paul, the author? (**He's in prison. When Paul first visited Philippi [Acts 16], he was promptly arrested and jailed. He escaped only because God provided an earthquake. Now Paul is in Rome, and once again in jail.) **How has this situation affected Paul's outlook and lifestyle?** (He is confident [v. 12]; he is telling everyone about Christ [v. 13]; he believes his imprisonment has been an encouragement to others [v. 14]; he is always ready to speak boldly for Christ [v. 20]; his one purpose is to "tell the Good News" [v. 27].)

Explain that Paul was giving a lesson, by example, in minority tactics. He was exhorting his readers to be fearless in telling others of Christ regardless of what their enemies might do; this would be the downfall of the enemies. Explain that Paul continues to outline these tactics in the next chapter. Instead of a survival kit, he gives a battle plan.

You may want to research in a commentary or two about the nature of Roman prisons. This would provide valuable background for the passage.

Battle Plan (10 minutes)

Now have group members turn to the next chapter and read Philippians 2:1-18. Give everyone a piece of paper and pencil and ask them to come up with a list of Paul's "battle plan." After a few minutes, have them present their lists. Put together a "master list" from the ones presented. The list should look something like this:

a. Love each other as Christians (v. 2)
b. Work together as Christians (v. 2)
c. Don't be selfish (v. 3)
d. Be humble, not trying to make a good impression on others (v. 3)
e. Be genuinely interested in others and in what they are doing (v. 4)
f. Be like Jesus—vv. (5-11)
g. Obey God with reverence (v. 12)
h. Realize that God is working in you (v. 13)
i. Don't complain or argue (v. 14)
j. Live clean, innocent lives (v. 16)
k. Hold out the "Word of Life" (v. 16)

Discuss each point briefly as it is given.

Make sure they make these lists and keep them. You will use them later.

WRAP-UP

Talk-to (5 minutes)

Say something like: **It seems to me that there needs to be quite a drastic change in our thinking. Just think of the tremendous effect we could have** on (your local high school) if we were to take seriously these instructions from God for facing our hostile environment. Instead of observing a small group of frightened, bickering individuals, the world would see a cohesive team of Christ-followers, confident, loving, unselfish, with one purpose: to tell others of Jesus. We've got every reason in the world to be confident! We have a concept that can't be whipped. Like one new Christian said to his friend right after reading Revelation, "I just skipped to the last chapter of the book—and we win!" That's exciting news.

Have group members look over their lists, pinpointing the minority tactic with which they need the most help right now. This tactic they should circle.

Prayer (3 minutes)

Close by spending a few moments in prayer. Encourage group members to ask God to forgive them and to give them the power to make the changes in their lives. Make this a time of silent prayer with one or two closing out loud.

Option for Further Study

Hand out the following "Minority Tactics Worksheet" and have group members look up one or two references each day during their quiet times for the next two weeks. They should write down next to the references how they apply to their lives as "minority group" students. Suggested applications in parentheses are for your use only.

Minority Tactics Worksheet
1. 1 Peter 4:4-5, 12-14 (Opposition isn't new.)
2. 2 Timothy 2:15-16 (Know God's message and avoid foolish discussions.)
3. Acts 17:22-34 (Paul was involved in an intellectual discussion, but he didn't argue.)
4. 1 Corinthians 1:18-20 (Many won't understand the Gospel.)
5. 1 Corinthians 2:1-5 (Jesus is the message.)
6. John 15:18-19 (You won't fit into the world's value system.)
7. Ephesians 1:18-19 (You have God's power in you; be confident.)
8. Ephesians 5:1-2, 8, 15-17 (Live like a Christian; love is the key.)
9. Ephesians 6:10-18 (It's a battle; be fully equipped.)
10. Philippians 2:14 (Avoid arguments.)
11. Matthew 6:33-34 (Don't worry; seek God first.)
12. Philippians 3:14 (Keep in mind your goal.)
13. Philippians 4:6 (Ask God to be with you and don't worry.)
14. 1 Corinthians 5:9-13 (Don't judge non-Christians; let God do that.)
15. Colossians 2:4-5 (Don't be fooled.)
16. 1 Peter 3:15; Colossians 4:5-6 (Be prepared to answer.)
17. Matthew 5:43-45 (Love and pray for those who put you down.)
18. Matthew 6:19-21 (Money isn't number one.)
19. 1 Corinthians 13:2 (Love is the key.)
20. Romans 12:21 (Overcome evil with good.)

Additional Resources

Out of the Salt Shaker (Rebecca Pippert, InterVarsity Press)
A very helpful book on witnessing—for students and leaders alike.

Giving Away Your Faith (Barry St. Clair, Victor Books)
An inductive study on evangelism that takes young people step by step through the process. A corresponding tract and follow-up booklet are also available so readers can practice presenting the Gospel.

FINDING FORGIVENESS IN CHRIST   1 JOHN 1:7–2:2

SESSION 10

NOT GUILTY!

WHAT CAN I DO ABOUT MY GUILT FEELINGS?

KEY CONCEPT	Most young people struggle with guilt and guilt feelings.
GOAL	This session will help your young people understand that total forgiveness is available through Jesus' death and resurrection and our faith in Him. They'll also be challenged to see that we have a responsibility to forgive others, just as we have been forgiven.
OVERVIEW	Guilt and guilt feelings are epidemic in our society, and young people are not immune. In fact, because of the demands on them from family, school, and church, combined with peer pressure and their own testing of moral boundaries, they can feel overwhelmed by guilt. In this session we will define guilt, identify its symptoms, and discuss what we can do about it. Too often Christian young people carry a load of debilitating guilt. They need to know and feel forgiveness—and then forgive others. This will be a very serious session.
TIME REQUIRED	30–45 minutes
MATERIALS CHECKLIST	Materials needed for basic session: _____ "Actors", newspapers, and other props (*Role Play*) _____ Chalkboard and chalk, or poster board and marker _____ *Forgiveness* worksheets _____ Pencils and pens _____ New Testaments Materials needed for optional activities: _____ Ping-Pong ball, quarter, and 3" x 5" card (*You're Gonna Catch It*) _____ Scratch paper (*Lists*)
JUNIOR HIGH ADAPTATION	This session covers an important topic for junior highers who are often engulfed by guilt feelings because of their emerging sex drives. For this session to be most effective, use *Lists* with only the "God" and "Parent" columns; do the *Role Play* with leaders or high school helpers; discuss the *Role Play*, and go directly to the two *Forgiveness* sheets; then wrap it up.

WARM-UP

Optional Openers

You're Gonna Catch It! (5–7 minutes)

The *title* of this game is directly related to our guilt feelings as we anticipate our punishment. Be sure to have a real penalty to heighten the tension. Choose participants who have healthy self-concepts.

This is a contest involving three or four people who must compete one at a time. Have the person stand in front of the crowd, facing them. Stand behind and throw a quarter, then a Ping-Pong ball, and finally a 3″ x 5″ card over his/her head. (Pause between items.) The idea is for the contestant to catch each item as it is thrown, before it hits the floor. He/she must catch two out of three or face a penalty. The quarter will be almost impossible to catch because it is hard to pick up visually, and it will drop straight down. The Ping-Pong ball, however, will be much easier, especially if you throw it gently, with a high arc. Hopefully, at this point the person will have caught one of the two, setting up anxiety and suspense for the last item. When you "throw" the card, it will float and drift slowly to the floor, but it will be difficult to catch. This is where this game becomes fun as the contestants try desperately to catch the card.

Lists (5–7 minutes)

The object of this activity is to identify potential guilt producing demands.

Give everyone an 8½″ x 11″ sheet of paper and have them divide one side into four columns. In the first column they should list all of the things that God wants them to do. In the second column, they should list the rules their parents have for them. The third column should contain what the church tells them to do. In the fourth column, they should write what the government expects from them. After a couple of minutes, compile these lists into a "master list" for the whole group. Some of the rules and expectations might include:

As you start compiling, you will inevitably trigger debates over individual sins (are these really wrong, etc.). Some of the questions will be unresolvable. The point of the exercise, however, is to help group members realize what is really wrong in God's eyes.

control my temper	do my chores
don't cheat in class	be in at curfew
play fair in sports	don't talk back
stop smoking	obey parents
stop fighting with brothers and sisters	don't lie
share my faith	worship
read my Bible	love my neighbor
pray more	tithe my income
love my enemies	confess my sins
stop swearing	obey traffic laws
keep in good health	pay taxes
keep from putting things off	obey age limits (drinking, etc.)
be more disciplined	don't take certain drugs
stop gossiping	vote
obey their commands	defend country

Role Play (7 minutes)

Choose these people carefully. They should be young people who will take this seriously and who can act. Line them up before the meeting and let them know what they will be doing, but *do not* give them the details of their roles. This should be a "fresh" role play.

Really emphasize this.

Explain that there will be a nonverbal role play performed by two of their friends who were chosen before the meeting. They will act out a scene without using any words, only gestures and facial expressions. Be sure to emphasize that this is not another humorous skit. Instead, it is a very serious illustration of what it feels like when you have wronged another person and you want to get it straightened out.

Tell everyone to be totally silent and then describe the situation out loud to your two participants. Here are the roles:

SON—Over a two-week period you have stolen nearly $200 from an envelope in which your dad was saving money for a doctor bill. Your mother has found out what you have done and has confronted you with the facts and informed your father. At first, your reaction was shame because you got caught. Now, however, it is beginning to bother you much more deeply. You've had a lot of differences with your dad, but he's not the worst father in the world. You have decided to return the money and ask for his forgiveness.

FATHER—When your wife told you what your son had done, you blew up saying, "That no good kid. He's had everything handed to him on a silver platter. He's soaked up the benefits of all my work and sacrifice—and this is the thanks I get"

But now you've cooled down a bit and have decided just to let your son stew for awhile. You don't care what kind of restitution he tries to make; you're not going to accept his apology. You want this to eat at him; maybe it'll teach him a lesson.

THE SCENE—Dad is in the living room reading the paper and the son is ready to go in and talk to him about it. Begin.

Allow the role play to continue just long enough for everyone to get into it and to feel the awkwardness and emotion. End it when both actors get to the peak of the performance.

Remind them that nobody speaks. They will have to communicate non-verbally.

If you would get a better performance using two girls, change the scene to a mother and a daughter.

Discussion (10 minutes)

Begin by talking about the role play. Ask the actors what they felt as they were playing their roles. Then ask the crowd what they were feeling during the role play and with which character they empathized most and why. Then say something like: **I'd like to stop a minute and draw the distinction between two words—*guilt* and *shame*. Shame is what we feel when we "get caught." We are embarrassed that we were too slow, too weak, or not clever enough. We don't feel as though we have done anything wrong really; we've simply gone against a social norm, a taboo of the group, and we'd like to cover up if we can. That's "shame."**

"Guilt," on the other hand, is the awareness of being at fault for what we have done—knowing that we have broken a trust or relationship with God or other people, or our ideals. A guilty person isn't as interested in trying to cover up as he or she is in repairing the breach, making restitution, and putting the pieces back together.

It may be helpful to distinguish between real guilt (when there has been a genuine offense) and false guilt (when we feel remorseful for having broken a taboo that was not really valid). Naturally, false guilt will evaporate when we understand the fallacy of the false taboo; real guilt will get only worse as we understand more about the gravity of our wrong.

Next, discuss how people act when they're guilty. Have group members describe the signs of guilt which they have seen in themselves, their parents, little kids, etc. List these on the board or a piece of posterboard. Here are a few possible answers:

- *Anger*—striking out at others because you feel trapped by the blame
- *Self-punishment*—turning the anger inward, cutting yourself down (but always hoping someone will contradict you and relieve the pressure)
- *Verbal aggression*—bad-mouthing someone else, being hypercritical and hostile towards others who often are unsuspecting
- *Depression*—feeling "blue," lousy, totally wiped-out
- *Apathy or boredom*—trying to stifle your feelings so severely that you shut down all systems; or else you try very hard to regain good graces, fail, and then drop out
- *Perfectionism*—determining not only to do better next time, but the absolute best, you create an ideal world, either in general (which dooms you to failure again) or in particular (at least your appearance, your desk, or your term paper will be perfect no matter what else happens).

WORKOUT

What Needs Forgiving? (13 minutes)

Distribute *Forgiveness Sheet #1* (see below) and instruct group members to fill it out as honestly as possible. For the last question, they will need their New Testaments.

Forgiveness Sheet #1

WHAT NEEDS FORGIVING?

1. Of what sin or shortcoming are you most aware?

2. Why that particular one?

3. How do you think God feels about that, right now?

4. What difference should 1 John 1:7–2:2 make regarding you, God, and your problem?

(A possible answer for the last question might be: I am a sinner but my sins will be forgiven if I confess them to Christ. Then not only will He forgive me, but He will also defend me before God.)

Give group members time to fill out the sheet. Then, have them look over what they have written while you give a short talk on the meaning of "sin" and "forgiveness." Say something like: **God never meant for Christians to walk around carrying a ton of guilt. What we have seen in 1 John is God's way of dealing with sin when it happens. We have to:**

1. *Call sin, "sin."* **We must be willing to quit rationalizing and justifying ourselves. It is sin, and God isn't pleased.**

2. *Recognize each sin as one for which Jesus died.* **Our right to feel forgiven is based on Christ's death. What about the specific sin you wrote on the worksheet? Try to imagine Christ dying for that one specifically. It's covered!**

3. *Ask God to forgive* **us, to clean us up, and to give us the power to change.**

4. *Forget it.* **God has said, "I will forgive their wickedness and will remember their sins no more" (Jeremiah 31:34). If a perfect God doesn't intend to think about it anymore, who are we to do so?**

Who Needs Forgiving? (10 minutes)

Introduce this sheet by saying something like: **Jesus told a story about guilt and forgiveness that highlights both sides of this exchange.** Then, have a student read Matthew 18:21–35.

Distribute *Forgiveness Sheet #2* (see next page) and allow time for group members to fill it out, carefully and honestly.

Forgiveness Sheet #2

WHO NEEDS FORGIVING?

1. To whom do you owe an apology? (List persons you have wronged.)

2. Why will it be difficult to make these situations right?

3. Who has really wronged you? How?

4. How would it affect that person if you let him/her know that you have forgiven and forgotten that problem.?

WRAP-UP

Talk-to (2 minutes)

Say something like: **There's a statement in the Bible that pretty well summarizes what we've discovered today. It's Ephesians 4:32, "Be kind and compassionate to one another, forgiving each other, just as in Christ God forgave you." Both sides of forgiveness are important. Offending others and God will be a fact of life as long as you are on this planet. With God's help you can conquer this problem, but you must claim God's forgiveness on your own when you sin. Forgiveness isn't a cheap conscience-quieter—not at all. Confessing sin means seeing just how serious it really is and then trusting God to forget it. Gratitude for His forgiveness will carry you a long way toward not allowing that sin to bother you again. And something happens to your relationships with other people when you feel forgiven. It allows you to become a *healer*, a "bridge," because you have seen God forgive and remove the sin in your life.**

Have group members close in prayer, individually, using the work sheets as their prayer guides. Encourage them to be totally honest with God.

If you have time, you may want to do the prayertime in groups allowing a few minutes for them to share with each other before they pray for each other.

Option for Further Study

Have group members keep track of their progress in the following areas:

1. Think about your friends. Have you exhibited any bad attitudes? Have you been critical of them? Have you cheated or lied to them? Don't wait. At your first chance, go to them and tell them you were wrong. Tell them you're sorry. Ask them to forgive you.

2. Go to your parent, your pastor, or a teacher. What is it that's standing in the way of a good relationship with these people? About what do you need to admit that you have been wrong? Go to them and say you're sorry.

   Say: **Use the back of the *Forgiveness* sheets to jot down your progress in these areas. We'll discuss them next time.**

Additional Resources

Guilt and Grace and *The Person Reborn* (Paul Tournier, Harper & Row)
These are excellent resources for the leader. This eminent psychologist emphasizes the reality of the forgiveness which can be ours through Christ.

UNDERSTANDING DEATH . . . AND LIFE   JAMES 4:13–15; PHILIPPIANS 1:20–26

SESSION 11

A MATTER OF LIFE AND DEATH

WHAT'S THE PURPOSE FOR MY LIFE?

KEY CONCEPT	Young people live as though they are "immortal," wasting time, squandering opportunities, taking chances, and putting off important decisions.
GOAL	This session will emphasize the truth that life is *short*, no matter how long a person lives and the importance of living for Christ.
OVERVIEW	This session will not be a morbid recital of sorrow and suffering. It will, however, emphasize the fact that eventually everyone has to die. Then, with this as the foundation, it will challenge young people to find their hope in Christ and to use their lives for Christ. Because death is such a difficult subject for young people to understand and accept, handle this content with sensitivity, especially if someone in the group has recently lost a loved one.
TIME REQUIRED	30–45 minutes
MATERIALS CHECKLIST	Materials needed for basic session: ____ Prizes and penalties (*Gone, but Not Forgotten*) ____ Paper and pencils (*Personal Epitaphs*) ____ New Testaments ____ Cards (*Commitment Cards*) Materials needed for optional activities: ____ Toilet paper (*Mummy Wrap*) ____ Copies of *The Last Thing We Talk About*
JUNIOR HIGH ADAPTATION	Junior high is not too early to begin to think seriously about death, but be careful. Most of your young teens will not have been to a funeral or spoken about death openly. Make sure that you do not come on too strong, scaring them in the process. Instead, lovingly push them to consider the reality of death and what it means to really live for Christ. The *Mummy Wrap* would be a good activity. Skip reading the actual epitaphs listed under *Personal Epitaphs*. Also, don't use *Pairs*. The rest of the session may be used as written.

WARM-UP

Optional Opener

Mummy Wrap (5–7 minutes)

This can be done with two people standing back-to-back or with teams. Give each pair a roll of toilet paper. They should race to see which pair can wrap themselves using the whole roll. The first couple done, wins.

This game takes a humorous look at an ancient burial custom. The idea is to get into the subject of death. Be sure to have a garbage bag handy for the toilet paper.

Gone, but Not Forgotten (6 minutes)

Have group members take the following quiz. Give a prize to whoever gets the most right answers. The correct answers are in parentheses. (Be sure you don't print them in the quiz!)

Match the person with the fact for which he or she is famous.

1. Bing Crosby (e.)
2. Elvis Presley (j.)
3. Jack Benny (f.)
4. Freddie Prinz (h.)
5. Bob Crane (d.)
6. Will Greer (b.)
7. Hubert Humphrey (k.)
8. Golda Meier (l.)
9. Leonid Brezhnev (c.)
10. John Paul I (g.)
11. Robert Shaw (a.)
12. John Lennon (n.)
13. Grace Kelly (o.)
14. John Belushi (m.)
15. Natalie Wood (p.)
16. Anwar Sadat (i.)

a. Jaws
b. Grandpa
c. Detente
d. Hogan
e. White Christmas
f. Violin
g. Pastor
h. Chico
i. Egypt
j. Graceland
k. Minnesota
l. Prime Minister
m. Blues Brothers
n. Strawberry Fields
o. Monaco
p. Native Wind

Update this quiz by adding other contemporary personalities who have died.

Personal Epitaphs (5 minutes)

Distribute paper and pencils and then introduce this activity by saying something like: **We've had some laughs over some of the things connected with dying, and often we would rather joke about death than to face it straight on. I'd like for us to pause for a few minutes to give some thought to death as *we* face it.** Explain that on the paper they have been given they should write:

1. Name in the middle of the paper.
2. Birth date a little above the name on the paper.
3. Today's date just a little below the name.
4. Under the date, a thought that would characterize his or her life.
5. A line around the information like this. . . .

Aug. 29, 1970

Oenog Fusser

Dec. 3, 1986

"He died too soon"

Have several persons scattered throughout the crowd ready to pass out paper and pencils at this point. When they have been passed out, proceed with *Personal Epitaphs*. It is important that you show how to do this as you explain it to them so hold up a paper with the completed picture. The goal of this activity is to get them to think seriously about how they would like to be remembered after they die.

Cite a local example if applicable and
appropriate.

Then say something like: **Yes, it's a tombstone with an epitaph on it. Kind of sobering, isn't it? Years ago it was very popular for persons to have an epitaph chiseled into their grave markers after they died. Some people wrote their own. Listen as I read some actual epitaphs:**

1. "Beneath this stone a lump of clay
   Lies Uncle Peter Daniels
   Who too early in the month of May
   Took off his winter flannels."
   Medway, Mass., 1746

2. "Here lies John Knott:
   His father was Knott before him,
   He lived Knott, died Knott
   Yet underneath this stone doth lie
   Knott christened, Knott begat
   And here he lies and still is Knott."
   Perthshire Churchyard

3. "It is so soon that I am done f[or]
   I wonder what I was begun for"
   For a child aged 3 weeks
   Chettenham Churchyard

4. "Here lies one who was nothi[ng]
   Piron's Epitaph

After this, have a number of young people share their "epitaphs." Some will be humorous; others quite serious.

WORKOUT

Discussion (8 minutes)

Explain that the life expectancy of today's teenager is about 73 years. But if your group members' high school population is about 1,000, it would not be unusual, according to death-rate statistics, for one or two students from the school to die this year. It could be from an accident. (Fourth leading cause of death in the U.S., vehicle related deaths make up nearly ½ of the accidental deaths in our country.) It could be from illness, suicide, or some other tragedy.

Read James 4:14, "Why, you do not even know what will happen to you tomorrow. What is your life? You are a mist that appears for a little while and then vanishes." Ask: **What does this verse tell us about life?** (Life is short; we can't even count on tomorrow.)

Emphasize the truth that *life is short no matter how long you live*. Whether people live to be 20 or 80, life is short, and eventually they will die.

Ask.: **What experiences have you had with deaths of friends, relatives, and others?** (Discuss answers.) **Are most people afraid to die? Why or why not? How do you feel right now, after confronting the idea of dying?**

Talk-to (4 minutes)

Say something like: **It is interesting and sobering to look at death and what it may mean to each of us. But at this point in our lives, the closest most of us have come to death is as the result of the death of a casual friend or a relative outside of our immediate families. Few of us have seen death within our own family or next door.**

Listen as I read from a book written by a man who has experienced the death of three of his children. The book is *The Last Thing We Talk About* by Joe Bayly. (Used by permission, David C. Cook Publishing Co.)

"The hearse began its grievous journey many thousands of years ago, as a litter made of saplings. Litter, sled, wagon, Cadillac: the conveyance has changed, but the corpse it carries is the same. Birth and death enclose man in a sort of parenthesis of the present. And the brackets at the beginning and end of life are still impenetrable. This frustrates us, especially in a time of scientific breakthrough and exploding knowledge that we should be able to break out of earth's environment and yet be stopped cold by death's unyielding mystery. Electroencephalogram may replace mirror held before the mouth, autopsies may become more sophisticated, cosmetic embalming may take the place of pennies on the eyelids and canvas shrouds, but death continues to confront us with its blank wall. Everything changes; death is changeless. We may postpone it, we may tame its violence, but death is still there waiting for us. Death always waits. The door of the hearse is never closed. Dairy farmer and sales executive live in death's shadow, with Nobel prize winner and prostitute, mother, infant, teen, and old man. The hearse stands waiting for the surgeon who transplants a heart as well as the hopeful recipient, for the funeral director as well as the corpse he manipulates. Death spares none."

Say: **Death has been a fear of man from the beginning of time. Many people ask, "Why, in an age of technology and scientific advancement are we still subject to death? Why haven't we conquered it? Why am I so afraid to die?" We are afraid of what is to come—the unknown—and afraid of the end of relationships on which our lives are based. So, in order to cope with death, we exclude it from our thinking. We are in the midst of a world that doesn't look to the truth about life or death. We postpone thinking about it until it happens.**

I'm not suggesting that we always think about death. That would be rather morbid. But it doesn't have to be an unsettled issue. We can be ready for it.

If there are non-Christian students present, this is a good opportunity for evangelism.

Bible Search (10 minutes)

Continue with the previous thought, asking group members how they think we can be ready for death. Answers may include taking a realistic view of your own mortality, knowing where you will be going after you die, making each day count, etc. Then have them turn to the following Scriptures and discuss them together. Be sure to bring out the points in the parentheses.

Hebrews 9:27—What does this say about death? (It is inevitable, and judgment follows.)
John 10:10; 14:6—What does this say about life? (Jesus is the source of life.)
John 3:16-17; 20:31—How can we have "eternal life?" (By believing in Christ)
John 11:25—How does "eternal life" relate to our lives right now? (We can have hope, knowing that we will live again after death.)

These are short passages with fairly obvious meanings so the discussion should move quickly. Add others if you wish.

Make the transition by saying; **God has provided a way by which we can prepare for the end of physical life. First it involves a spiritual life that can begin right now and never end. And second, He has promised a resurrection to life with Him. I hope you have settled this issue of belief in Christ so that you are ready to die. If not, there can be no better time than right now.**

Next, have everyone turn to Philippians 1:20-26 and read the passage silently. Then ask: **What is Paul's main thought here?** (Vs. 21: dying would be great because

List all of their answers and press for very practical ways that they can live for Christ. It would also be helpful for them to imagine what this phrase must have meant for Paul. If discussion is slow, ask, "How would you change your life if you learned you had only six months to live?"

Make sure they take this very seriously.

Watch out for those who can't find a suitable partner or for whom this is too threatening. Have adult leaders "free" to meet with them.

he would go to heaven, but living means opportunities to live for Christ.) **How can we live for Christ?** (Discuss this for awhile, listing their answers.)

WRAP-UP

Commitment Cards (5 minutes)

Hand out 3" x 5" cards and have group members write their names on the top. Then, have them spend a minute or two considering what two or three actions they should take to begin to "live for Christ." As they think and pray about this, offer various suggestions (love people, serve the needy, use time better, obey and respect parents, use talents for God's glory, change certain behaviors, etc.). Then, after they have decided on their changes, have them write these on their cards. Then, have them hold the cards quietly until everyone has finished. Summarize briefly what you have discussed during the session:

1. **Life is so very short—every minute should count**
2. **God has given us life, time, talent, friends, and other loved ones, but we often take these for granted.**
3. **Though everyone has to die, we can have hope through faith in Jesus Christ.**
4. **We should make our lives count for Christ through our attitudes, goals, words, and actions.**

Pairs (5 minutes)

Have everyone find a partner—someone they know fairly well. (Involve adult helpers in this also.) Have partners spend a few minutes talking through what they wrote on their cards and then praying for each other. Then they should swap cards and commit to pray for the other person each day for the next two weeks.

Options for Further Study

Buy copies of *The Last Thing We Talk About* by Joe Bayly and discuss the content.

Go through the stages of dealing with crisis or grief as outlined by Elizabeth Kubler-Ross in her famous work, *On Death and Dying*.

Additional Resources

The Last Thing We Talk About (Joe Bayly, David C. Cook)
This book is extremely well written and is packed with content. It is inspirational and practical and is good reading for high school age and above.

Is God Really Fair? (Dick Dowsett, Moody Press)
This short volume answers questions for young Christians. Chapter 11, "She Died—and I Loved Her," would be helpful.

SESSION 12

THAT'S A NO-NO!

HOW DO I KNOW HOW GOD WANTS ME TO ACT?

KEY CONCEPT	Christian young people are susceptible to peer pressures and are often confused about what they should or shouldn't do.
GOAL	This session will help your young people evaluate whether their actions are consistent with God's will and will show them how to discover the biblical principles on which they can base positive Christian behavior.
OVERVIEW	Young people are subjected to many pressures and influences. From all sides people are telling them how to act—peers, teachers, parents, society, church. Most *Christian* young people want to do what *God* wants, but they can become easily confused in the midst of all these voices. Of course *God's* will must take precedence over all the other influences; but how can a person know what God wants? This is an important question to answer because the Bible does not contain specific instructions for each and every occasion. This session, therefore, will emphasize specific biblical principles on which group members should base their behavior. After discovering these principles, be sure to emphasize how they are applied in daily living.
TIME REQUIRED	30-45 minutes
MATERIALS CHECKLIST	Materials needed for basic session: ____ Paper and pencils (*Party*) ____ *Taboo or Not Taboo* sheets ____ Tapes/records and script (*Voices*) ____ Chalkboard and chalk, or poster board and marker (*Diagram*) ____ New Testaments ____ Paper (*Assignment*) Materials needed for optional activities: ____ Balloons and strings (*Balloon Wallow*) ____ Script and flag (*George's Story*)
JUNIOR HIGH ADAPTATION	This session is more appropriate for high schoolers but it is an important concept for junior highers to consider. Just be sure to scale down to their level the discussion, the *Taboo or Not Taboo* chart, and the *Study*. In other words, keep the discussion brief, list only three or four items on the chart, and choose specific verses from the longer passages listed in *study*. All of the games should work well as should the *Assignment*. Be sure to check up on their assignments when you said you would.

WARM-UP

Optional Openers

Balloon Wallow (5 minutes)

The object of this game is to have fun and to picture how we often feel when pressured by obligations and requests on all sides. Choose people who are self-confident and won't mind rolling on the floor in front of the group. This can also be done as a team competition with representatives from the teams.

Choose two or three students and tie several balloons to each of them—on arms, knees, neck, anywhere. Leave 24 inches or so of string on each balloon so that the balloons are not easy to pin down. The first one to burst all his or her balloons without using hands or teeth wins.

George's Story (7 minutes)

The object of this game is to have fun and to illustrate how we often "jump" when others "call the shots."

Divide the group into give sections. Each section should react when their assigned word is read, as follows:

"George"—salute and say "ah-ha!"
"Soldier"—stamp feet and clap hands
"Betsy Ross" and any other women's name—whistle
"Country"—shout "Whoopee!"
"Flag"—shout "Hurrah!"

Here is the script that you read outloud:

Once upon a time in a faraway COUNTRY named the United States of America, there lived a man named GEORGE WASHINGTON. He was a SOLDIER and his wife's name was MARTHA. He was named for the little boy who couldn't tell a cherry tree about the cutting down lie. GEORGE WASHINGTON was called "The Father of his COUNTRY," because he discovered it in 1492. One day GEORGE and Alexander the Great, who was a SOLDIER and married to MAID MARIAN, (he was called "The Great" because of his famous words, "I regret that I have but one life to give for my COUNTRY") were out riding in GEORGE'S new Buick.

They were listening to a radio program all about the French FLAG. GEORGE looked very sad and said, "Gee, ain't it fierce that our COUNTRY ain't got no FLAG? Alexander the Great said, "Gee, ain't it fierce?"

They rode over to Coney Island for a hot dog and met a SOLDIER and his girlfriend, PIEZASTER. He was a friend of GEORGE who was such a good fighter that they called him Jack Dempsey. Jack, who was married to GRETA GARBO, was talking to GEORGE about the fact that their COUNTRY ain't got no FLAG. The SOLDIER said, "Gee, ain't it fierce? What shall we do?"

They all thought and thought, and suddenly GEORGE said, "I have it! I'll ask BETSY ROSS about it."

When they got to BETSY'S home, GEORGE WASHINGTON said, "BETSY, our COUNTRY ain't got no FLAG."

BETSY said, "Gee, ain't it fierce? A COUNTRY with as good SOLDIERS as Jack Dempsey and the other Marines oughta have a FLAG. I know, GEORGE, I'll make one." And she did. And just to prove that this incident is true, here is the FLAG that BETSY made (pull out a flag and wave it) because GEORGE and the SOLDIER wanted our COUNTRY to have a FLAG.

Party (8 minutes)

Arrange the group in a circle (or at least in a configuration where paper can be passed from person to person) and pass out pencils and sheets of 8½"×11" paper. At the top of the papers have them write, "I went to the party and . . ." Next, explain that when you tell them to start, they should begin to write a story with that as the opening line. Encourage them to be creative. They should write until you shout, "pass it on," at which time they should pass the paper to the person on the right. Then they should continue the story that they have received and write until you say, "pass it on" again. Continue this process for about five minutes, allowing about 30-45 seconds for each bit of writing; then have them pass the stories two more times and read them silently. Finish by having a few of the "best" stories read out loud.

You may want to give them a little more time to write as the game progresses because each time they will have to read a longer story. The object of this game is to set the stage for discussing what happens at a party or other peer-pressure situation.

Discussion (3 minutes)

Ask about how realistic these "party stories" were. Some will be totally "off the wall," but there may be a few realistic statements or situations (i.e. pressure to drink, etc.). Then ask: **When someone suggests that you have a big weekend, get drunk, mess around with girls or guys, why do you respond as you do? Notice that I didn't say, "How do you respond?" I'm asking, "Why do you respond as you do?"**

Allow time for some answers. Try not to comment on them. You will have time to get into this later.

Voices (4 minutes)

End the discussion and have everyone turn over the "party story" papers and get ready to write on the back. Tell them that in a few minutes they will hear a message and that they should write down as much of the message as they can. (Before the meeting set up two or three tape or record players around the room, or get young people to sing or talk, or combine noisemakers.) At this time, begin all the tapes. It will, of course, be chaotic; but while the tapes are playing, etc., read a story to the group. After about two minutes, stop everything and ask what they wrote on their papers. Explain that this was a demonstration of how we often feel when surrounded by people who are trying to tell us what to do or what to believe. With so much noise, it is difficult to know how or to whom to listen. Then ask: **What are the "voices" in your life? Who is trying to influence you?** (Their answers may include friends, rock musicians, parents, teachers, politicians, and others.) Summarize by explaining that it can be confusing to know just exactly what to do in certain situations.

The object of this is to experience what it's like to be subjected to a torrent of voices in our lives. Advance preparation is important.

Don't spend too much time on this— the purpose is to set-up the "Taboo or Not Taboo Chart."

WORKOUT

Taboo or Not Taboo (8 minutes)

Hand out the *Taboo or Not Taboo* sheets (sample printed at the end of the session) and explain that this chart should help them answer these questions. Then ask for specifics to list in column one. In other words, "What are you being told you *should* or *should not* do?" This list will not be exhaustive, but be sure the examples are both positive and negative and from a variety of areas of life. The list could include witnessing, drinking (and not drinking), studying, doing drugs, obeying parents, and others.

Make sure they have something hard on which to write (books, magazines, etc.).

Next, go to the second column entitled, "What do I think?" Have them think through and record their views on the listed items. Then do the same for the third column, "What do others think?"

When you finish the third column say something like: **When we consider "What does God want?," we have a little more difficulty determining the answers. Let me give you an illustration that should be of some help.**

Diagram (5 minutes)

Draw the diagram *as* you explain it.

Put the following diagram on the chalkboard or a piece of poster board and explain it carefully saying something like: **God communicates Himself and His desires to us in a general way through the world around us. But when it comes to specific matters in our lives, He has promised to help. That help comes through His Word (the Bible) and His Work (His activities in our lives). The Holy Spirit is active in this communication process, and the Holy Spirit will not lead in a way contrary to what God has already revealed in the Bible—the objective record of God's nature and desires.**

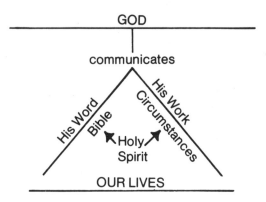

Study (8 minutes)

Explain that together you will look at some passages in the Bible which give principles on which we can base decisions like the ones listed.

Make sure that group members understand each principle before you move on. *After* you decide on the principle(s), have them write.

Have everyone read Romans 14:1-23, silently, looking for the principles. Then ask group members to explain the principles that they found. Summarize each principle and have the young people write them on the back of their *Taboo or Not Taboo* sheets. For this passage the principles would include: We must be careful not to offend a "weaker" Christian, and we must not judge others by our own standards (whether we are "weak" or "strong").

Repeat the process with 1 Corinthians 10:23-33. Point-out these principles: As Christians, we may do anything, but it should be useful and/or constructive; we must always think of the welfare of others (vv.23-24). We should do all to the glory of God; that is, our motivation must be right (v.31). We must do nothing which would hinder another person's salvation (v.32-33).

Repeat with 1 Peter 1:22 and 3:8-12. Emphasize these principles: Everything we do must be judged by the "law of love," and we should especially love our brothers and sisters in Christ. To reinforce this, have someone read 1 Corinthians 13:4-7. Explain that this kind of love is not a soupy, warm, fuzzy feeling. It is *responsible action*.

Ask if there are any other biblical principles group members can remember which would be applicable. Explain that the Bible is *filled* with God's principles to help us.

WRAP-UP

Individual Application (4 minutes)

Make sure they take their time and do this right. They should not worry about getting through the whole list.

Referring back to the *Taboo or Not Taboo* charts, ask for suggestions for a couple of answers in column four, "What does God think about it?" to make sure they under stand how to *apply* the biblical principles to specific situations. Then ask them to take a few minutes on their own to fill in the rest of the answers.

Summary (3 minutes)

Explain that this is a day-by-day, moment-by-moment process of being sensitive to the Holy Spirit about certain areas of our lives, apply the principles to those specific situations, and then *acting* on what we know. This is how we build *convictions*, not just our own opinions or reflections of someone else's ideas. Emphasize that it is not enough to want to do what God wants—that's the starting point—but we must read His Word to find out what He wants. And it is not enough to read the Bible, we must make specific applications to our lives. It is not enough to make applications, we must act, obeying and changing to conform to His will. Real convictions result in changed lives.

Assignment (2 minutes)

Have group members review their *Taboo or Not Taboo* charts and choose one or two items that need changing. Then pass out paper and have them design a simple "action plan" which they will use prayerfully and carefully during the next week to make the necessary changes. Offer possible steps that can be included in these plans and let them know that you and other adult helpers are available for personal counsel.

Close with prayer asking for wisdom and guidance daily.

Option for Further Study

Give group members assignments of talking over *all* the items, in depth, with their pastor or another Christian adult, asking for their help in discovering other relevant biblical principles and in making specific applications of the principles already listed.

Additional Resource

Decisions! Decisions! Decisions! (Steve Lawhead, Victor Books)
This is a very practical book, geared to high school students. It emphasizes knowing how to make the right, God-centered decisions. This would also be a good resource for a continuing small group study on this subject.

TABOO OR NOT TABOO CHART
n the far left column, list things that you've been told to do, or told not to do.

TABOO-OR-NOT-TABOO CHART

Taboos-or-not-taboos	What do I think?	What do others think?	What does God want?

When you reprint this, be sure to leave room for their answers—you also may want to list more than ten items.

BUILDING SOLID FRIENDSHIPS   SELECTED PASSAGES

SESSION 13

JUST FRIENDS

HOW CAN I BE A TRUE FRIEND?

KEY CONCEPT	One of our basic needs is to love and to be loved; and yet most people have very few deep, caring relationships. Young people are no exception; in fact, the problem may be even more severe for them as they mature and strive for independence.
GOAL	This session will help your young people grasp basic principles of establishing and maintaining deep and solid relationships.
OVERVIEW	Young people are surrounded by people—family, classmates, teammates, and others. In this sea of faces, however, they often find very few close friends. Because they are pushing for independence, parents and siblings are set aside. Because they are discovering their sexuality, members of the opposite sex are mysterious and often intimidating. And because they are struggling with their own problems, peers become strangers. It is not unusual, therefore, for high school students to feel lonely, alienated, and isolated. This session will focus on how to establish and build relationships with family, dates, adults, peers, and, especially, friends. Obviously this cannot be an exhaustive study—a seminar or continuing small group could carry it further—but we will be laying the foundation. As you teach, be sensitive to the hurts beneath the surface and be ready to bring love and healing.
TIME REQUIRED	30-45 minutes
MATERIALS CHECKLIST	Materials needed for basic session: ____ Paper and pencils (*How Do They Rate?*) ____ Chalkboard and chalk, or poster boards and marker ____ *Relationship Evaluation* sheets Materials needed for optional activities: ____ Questions and prices (*Best Friends Quiz*) ____ Newspapers or towels (*Know Your Friend or Else*) ____ Assignments (*Togetherness*)
JUNIOR HIGH ADAPTATION	Use the session as it is, but be ready for discussion at a more superficial level. Also, select specific Bible verses from the longer passages.

WARM-UP

Optional Openers

Best Friends Quiz (8 minutes)

Ask for two girls and two boys who are good friends to volunteer to play this game which is patterned after "The Newlywed Game." Send one of each out of the room. Then ask boy-number-one and then girl-number-one the following questions (or make up your own quiz):

1. Would (s)he loan you his last dollar if it meant (s)he couldn't buy a present for his girlfriend (or her boyfriend)?
2. Is your friend faithful to his girlfriend (or her boyfriend)?
3. Would (s)he steal your girlfriend (or boyfriend) from you if (s)he got the chance?
4. Does your friend pity you, envy you, or admire you?

Bring in the other friends—boy-number-two and girl-number-two—one at a time, and ask how they think their partner-friends answered the previous questions. The set of friends to match correctly the most answers, wins.

The object of this game is to have fun and to focus on friendship. Add other questions if these are not appropriate for your friends. You may want to have a penalty for the losing friends.

Know Your Friend or Else (7 minutes)

Arrange everyone into circles of 10 or 11 and give them a couple of minutes to learn everyone's first name. Then choose one person in each group to stand in the center of the circle with a rolled up newspaper in his hand. The game begins when a designated person in the circle yells his name and someone else's name in the circle. That person whose name was called second must then say his own name again and then someone else's name before the person in the middle hits him on the head with the newspaper. When a person gets hit before he says the two names, he changes places with the person in the center. Example: John-Mary, Mary-Sally, Sally-whack! (they change places). The person who has just been in the middle and has become one of those in the circle, begins the process again.

The object of this game is to have fun and to help members learn each others' names. Obviously, it won't work in smaller groups. Towels can be used instead of newspapers.

How Do They Rate? (6 minutes)

Distribute papers and pencils to everyone. Ask them to write down the names of 20 "friends" on the left side of the paper. These do not have to be close friends and may include relatives, adults, fellow students, and others. Next have them rate their relationship with each person to the right of each name. Here is the rating scale: 5 = a great relationship; 4 = good; 3 = OK; 2 = poor; 1 = bad. Make sure that they understand that this is how *they* feel about the relationship, not you or anyone else. After they have rated all their people, have them total the points and then divide by 20 to get the average rating. After this has been done, find out the range of most of their totals.

Make sure they have 20 names. This may be difficult for some, so be ready to offer suggestions. Make sure they understand that this list will not be picked up or discussed in depth with the group. They should be honest.

Say something like: **Most of us would have to admit that our relationships need work. Remember, this rating was only of your friends; it did not include acquaintances or "enemies." And it was how you felt about the friendship, not according to a standard of what friendships should be. Even if you had a "perfect" score of 100, you would probably say that many of those relationships needed work. How was your total? Was it close to 100 . . . or close to 10? How many of your relationships did you rate 4 or 5? How many 1 or 2? And what was your average? Where did your relatives, especially your mom and dad fit in? Of course this was not a scientific study, but it does give us an indication of where we stand with our relationships.**

Discussion (5 minutes)

This is an important discussion, but don't let it drag or take a position yourself. Acknowledge each contribution and move on.

Say: **Think about your best friend in grade school. Without using any names, describe him or her.** (Note: look for facts about where they lived, how they got to know each other, what their personalities were like, etc.) Ask: **What does it take to build a friendship?** Common interests, spending time together, caring about each other, listening to each other, etc.) **How does God fit into your friendships?** He's a common interest; He gives us the ability to love, etc.)

WORKOUT

Talk-to (4 minutes)

Explain that during this session you will be discussing two of life's three basic relationships. Sketch the following illustration on a chalkboard or poster board, emphasizing each relationship with the drawing of each arrow.

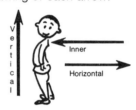

Vertical = one's relationship with God
Horizontal = one's relationship with others
Inner = one's relationship to oneself (This will not be covered in this session.)

Say something like: **Man is a social being. We are seldom by ourselves. It is our nature to do almost everything in groups—families, church groups, cliques, clubs, fraternities, and groups of friends. Because this is true, any conflict in these three basic relationship areas directly affects the others.**

If you are full of inner conflict, it usually affects your behavior toward other people.

If you are at odds with God, then you probably can't stand yourself.

Jesus said it was impossible to maintain a right relationship to God unless everything was right with your fellow men (others). Doesn't the "Lord's Prayer" have something to say about that?

Putting it all together, it looks like this. A good and healthy relationship with God leads to a good relationship with yourself which leads to a good relationship with others . . . and vice versa. These three relationships are intertwined."

Vertical Study (8 minutes)

This will be a review for most, but it is important to cover this ground. Assign the verses to various young people and have them read aloud. After each passage, have the reader summarize its message. Then show how it fits into the following outline.

1. Man's original relationship with God the Father was destroyed by sin **Isaiah 59:2; Romans 6:23.**
2. Jesus Christ, God's Son, took our place—the only candidate who could—to make possible the return to a right relationship to the Father **Romans 5:1, 6, 8-10.**

3. The Holy Spirit will live in us and provide God's power and Christlikeness **Acts 1:8; Galatians 5:22-23.**
4. We must keep the communication and ''power'' channels open with God through being honest with Him about our sins **1 John 1:9.**

Horizontal Study (10 minutes)

Explain that you are now ready to look at "horizontal relationships"; because when our relationships with God are in order, He will give us additional insight and understanding as to how to relate properly to others (1 John 4:7-11).

Draw the following illustration showing how their horizontal relationships involve the world of youth on one hand and the adult world on the other.

ADULT WORLD - - - - - - - - YOU - - - - - - - - WORLD OF YOUTH
   Parents   Brothers
   Clergy   Sisters
   Teachers   Classmates
   Neighbors   Friends
   Employers

Assign the following verses and ask how they relate to these various relationships. Make sure that each student has at least one verse to look up (with a large crowd, break into two's or three's for each passage). *Ephesians 5:1-2; 3-4; 19-21; 6:1-3; 5-9; 18; Hebrews 13:17; 1 Corinthians 13:4-7; Romans 12:9-10; Galatians 5:22-23; 6:10; Philippians 2:2-4; John 13:34-35; James 2:1-4; 1 Thessalonians 4:9-10.* Next, have the group list some of the ways in which *healthy* and *unhealthy* horizontal relationships are demonstrated in daily life. Here are some possibilities.

Healthy
  1. Love and care
  2. Helpful
  3. Dependable
  4. Reliable
  5. Tolerant
  6. Thankful
  7. Consistent temperament
  8. Respectful
  9. Honest
 10. Sympathetic

Unhealthy
  1. Selfish
  2. Gossip
  3. Flippant
  4. Ambivalent
  5. Jealous
  6. Envying
  7. Cheating others
  8. Bitterness
  9. Lying
 10. Griping

You may want to add selected Proverbs to this list.

These answers may be given out loud, but they also could be noted when you make the ''unhealthy'' and ''healthy'' lists.

Jot down one or two of these characteristics to stimulate contributions from the group.

WRAP-UP

Relationship Evaluation (5 minutes)

Explain that group members should evaluate the important relationships in their lives. Pass out the *Relationship Evaluation* sheets (printed at the end of this session) and urge them to be honest. At this time they should *not* fill in the two ''improvements'' columns. Also, for the categories of ''friends,'' ''classmates,'' and ''neighbors,'' they should think of one person.

Talk-to (2 minutes)

After they have completed this first step of their *Relationship Evaluation* sheets, summarize briefly a couple of the key points that you discovered together from the two ''studies.'' Then say something like: **God wants the best for us. He wants**

healthy relationships. And the beauty of knowing Him is that the vertical relationship we have with Him doesn't make it more difficult to have loving relationships with others. In fact, it works the other way around. God not only tells us to 'love,' but He also says, "I'll help you love." In Philippians 2:13 we are told that God is working _in_ us, giving us both the desire and the ability to do what He wants.

Action (5 minutes)

Have group members look again at their _Relationship Evaluation_ sheets and complete the columns calling for improvement—the "date" and "how-to" columns. Challenge them to do what they have written and then close in prayer.

Options for Further Study

Offer to have a continuing small group study, using one of the books listed in _Additional Resources,_ about how to build friendships.

Togetherness—For those who are interested, give "friendship building" assignments. They should find a friend and do one of the following together: prepare a slide and tape show for the rest of the group on "Friends"; create a short play about friendship; interview five older people about their greatest friendships and what made them great; create three or four symbols of friendship; and others.

Additional Resources

Real Friends (Barbara B. Varenhorst, Harper and Row)
A very practical volume on the basics of friendship—meeting people, listening, being sensitive to the other person's needs, and others. It is very helpful for those lonely students who desperately want friendship.

"What Difference Does It Make?" (Editors of _Campus Life_)
This is a special, pass-along issue of _Campus Life_ magazine which has an excellent section on friendship.

Friend to Friend (J. David Stone and Larry Keefauver, Group Books)
An easy-to-read and -use paperback on how to help a friend work through a problem.

When you reprint this, be sure to leave room for answers.

RELATIONSHIP EVALUATION
Rate yourself on the following:

1—At present, everything's all right.
2—I'm honestly working on it.
3—Bad news!

VERTICAL RELATIONSHIPS
☐ The best you can, rate your relationship to God the Father. Is there proper Father-son/daughter harmony between you?

☐ Have you made allowance for the function of God the Holy Spirit in your life? Are there areas in which He does not have control?

☐ What is your relationship to God the Son, Jesus Christ? Do others see his reflection in your life?

HORIZONTAL RELATIONSHIPS

Rate your relationship to your—	Where necessary, I will attempt improvement by Date:	This is how I can improve
☐ Brother (s)	_____	_____
☐ Sister (s)	_____	_____
☐ Friends	_____	_____
☐ Classmates	_____	_____
☐ Clergyman	_____	_____
☐ English Teacher	_____	_____
☐ Neighbors	_____	_____
☐ Employer	_____	_____
☐ Parents	_____	_____
☐ Others	_____	_____

UNDERSTANDING "CHRISTIAN" DATING   SELECTED PASSAGES

SESSION 14

DATES TO REMEMBER

HOW SHOULD A CHRISTIAN ACT ON A DATE?

KEY CONCEPT	In a culture of sexual innuendos and expectations, young people can be confused about "dating," its place and purpose, and how to act on a date.
GOAL	This session will emphasize the responsibility that each person in a relationship has for the other and for the necessity of acting in love.
OVERVIEW	Dating is an adolescent ritual filled with expectations, pressures, self-doubts, and anxieties. Young people are expected to date by society, teachers, parents, and, most important, their peers. But dating is not easy, especially when it is surrounded by romantic idea of love and sexual feelings. Christian young people are not immune to these problems and questions; in fact, they may be intensified because of the additional moral factors. This session, therefore, will emphasize what the Bible says about Christian relationships, focusing on the purpose of dating and encouraging young people to "relax" in their relationships, to build friendships, to get to know others, and to be truly "loving" in all they do. Remember, this session is not "exhaustive." It does not answer every dating issue. So be ready to follow through with personal conversations or with continuing group discussions on this important topic.
TIME REQUIRED	30-45 minutes
MATERIALS CHECKLIST	Materials needed for basic session: ____ "Top 40" song list (*Love Songs*) ____ Pencils and paper ____ Role play situations (*The Turndown*) ____ Script (*Dream Date*) ____ New Testaments ____ Chalkboard and chalk, or poster board and marker Materials needed for optional activities: ____ Grapefruit and prizes (*Grapefruit Pass*) ____ Straws (*First Kiss*) ____ Participants and blindfolds (*Blind Date*)
JUNIOR HIGH ADAPTATION	Instead of the printed role plays for *The Turndown*, write role plays (and discussion questions) which depict typical junior high dating situations (e.g. "pairing up" at a party, trying to tell someone how you feel about her/him without making a fool of yourself, etc.).

WARM-UP

Optional Openers

Grapefruit Pass (5 - 8 minutes)

These do not have to be dating couples. The goal of this game is to have fun and to get them thinking about "couples." If the grapefruit falls, pick it up and have them try again. *Remember,* no hands allowed.

Choose three couples to compete. Bring them to the front and seat each couple side-by-side in folding chairs. Explain that the contest is to see which couple can successfully pass a grapefruit from one person to the other, from a sitting position, held neck to chin. They may not rise off the chairs, move the chairs, or use their hands. Award a prize to the winning couple (such as a box of candy).

First Kiss (6 - 7 minutes)

You can use either sex for your volunteers, but be sure they are older students who can take a joke. After each one says the extemporaneous line, and everyone laughs, have him or her sit down and bring in the next person. After all three have finished, explain to them what their lines meant. The goal of this game is to have fun and to focus on one aspect of dating.

Choose three contestants and have them leave the room (tell them only that they will compete in the next game). Take a long and a short broom straw and give them to the biggest person in the room to hold. They should be held so you can't tell which is the short straw. Then clue-in the audience. A contestant will come in, will be instructed to choose the shorter of the two straws (thinking this is the beginning of a game). The person holding the straws will, however, refuse to let go of the straw he has chosen. The words the "victim" says after that are then to be taken as the words this person said as he was attempting his first kiss. (e.g. "If you don't give it to me, I'm going to let you have it!")

Love Songs (7 minutes)

The goal of this game is to have fun and to start them thinking about the cultural influences concerning sex and dating. Don't spend too much time discussing this; it is only warm-up.

Pick up a copy of the Top-40 songs from a record store. Divide into three or four teams and explain that you are going to have a game that is a cross between "charades," "scavenger hunt," and "Name that Tune." Have each team send a representative to the front and give them each a sheet of paper and a pen. Explain that you are going to whisper to them the name of a popular song, the title of which they must get their teams to guess. At your signal, then, they are to run back to their teams and draw a picture which represents the song. *They may not speak or draw any letters or numbers.* The first team to guess the correct title wins that round. Continue for seven or eight rounds, using different team representatives each time. Only use love songs.

After you have declared the winning team ask:

1. What did these songs have in common?
2. What popular songs can you think of that don't talk about love or sex?
3. Why is this the theme of most songs?
4. Describe the kind of love pictured in these songs.

Dream Date (5 minutes)

The idea here is to turn their thoughts specifically to dating. As you hear the words that they offer, be sure to use ones which will make the descriptions funny and "clean."

Don't tell group members the title of this activity. Simply ask them for the various parts of speech listed in the blanks in the script. Encourage them to be creative; this should be fun. After you have filled in all the blanks, read the title and their group description of the "Dream Date."

Script: "My dream guy is really _____ (adjective). His _____ (noun) is _____ (adj.); his eyes are like _____ (plural noun); his teeth are like _____ (plural noun); and his _____ (plural noun) ripple when he flexes them. And he is so talented. I love the way he _____ (verb), and he can _____ (verb) like a _____ (noun). His personality is so _____ (adj.). Actually, my dream guy is most like _____ (name of someone in the room)."

"My dream girl is really _____ (adjective) looking. Her skin is so _____ (adj.), and her _____ (number) eyes are like _____ (plural noun). Her voice sounds like _____ (sound) to my ears whenever she says _____ (exclamation). Her _____ (adj.) _____ (color) hair flows down her back. But perhaps her most outstanding feature is her _____ (adj.) _____ (body part). She has a wonderful _____ (verb ending in "ing") talent. Actually, my dream girl is most like _____ (name of someone in the room)."

The Turndown (7 minutes)

Choose two students or adult helpers to role play this common situation. The girl has just been called by a boy in whom she is not interested at all. He asks her out, and she turns him down with a "creative excuse." He is persistent, however, and continues to ask for other dates; but she continues to find "reasons" to say no. Stop the role play and discuss it briefly, using the following questions:

1. **Girls, have you ever been in this situation? What did you do? What are some of the excuses that you have given? Why didn't you just tell him your real feelings? What attracts you to a boy?**
2. **Boys, has this ever happened to you? How did you feel? Can you think of any better way for a girl to turn you down? Is it difficult for you to ask a girl for a date? Why? What attracts you to a girl?**

Obviously this focuses directly on dating. Watch out, however, because they may want to discuss this for quite awhile. Keep the discussion concise, make your points, and move on.

WORKOUT

Love Lists (7 minutes)

Give everyone a piece of paper and a pencil or pen. Have them write down, as many as they can imagine, ways to express love to another person. Share and compare the lists, and then ask:

1. **Which of these "ways" are realistic?**
2. **Which of them apply to parents? . . . brothers and sisters? . . . girlfriend or boyfriend? . . . God?**
3. **What's the difference between "like" and "love?"**
4. **What's the difference bewteen "love" and "lust?"**

This is an important discussion, but don't let it drag. Watch for any differences in how they perceive love for God, a girl/boyfriend, and parents. Also, make sure they think through these last two questions.

Discussion (5 minutes)

Use this discussion to pull together some of the elements of the meeting. How much time you need will depend on the previous discussions, but keep this concise. Explain that dating has often been called, "cruel and unusual punishment" because of the anxieties it causes and the pressures under which it puts us. We play all sorts of "dating games," trying to get asked by the right boy or trying to get that special girl to like us. The truth of the matter is that many young people go through high school without having even one date.

Ask: What should be the purpose of dating? (To meet members of the opposite sex, to build friendships, to know what you want in a marriage partner, etc.) How can you fulfill these purposes in dates? (By having fun together, maybe doing things in groups, finding mutual interests, sharing a variety of experiences, etc.) How should Christians be different in their dates? (It's important to keep lust out of the picture, trying to build

Use these questions as "guides." In other words, don't move down the list, one after another. The idea is to have them think through dating, thoroughly.

a constructive relationship instead of "using" each other.) How does love fit into the dating picture? (Love can be an attitude of caring and respect—not just feeling excited about a certain person. Love can grow as a friendship grows.) Why is there so much sexual pressure in dating? (The "world" portrays sex and love as going hand-in-hand. There is a big emphasis on pleasing yourself no matter what. TV, movies, ads—all of these stress sex, even for teenager.)

Bible Study (6 minutes)

Explain that though the New Testament does not deal specifically with dating, it does give us guiding principles. Then, have various students read the verses listed below. After each one, together determine the principle which is being taught. List these on the chalk or a piece of poster board.

1. Romans 12:3-8—We must have a proper view of ourselves. (When we think too highly of ourselves, we will tend to use people to meet our needs and to demand things from them.)

2. Galatians 5:13-14—Christians are free, but free to serve each other, not to hurt each other. We should be guided by love.

3. Galatians 6:2—Christians should help each other do what is right.

4. Ephesians 4:29—We must watch how we talk to each other, using words to build, not tear down.

Be immitators of God

5. Ephesians 5:1-7:—We must stay away from any kind of sexual immorality.

6. Philippians 1:9-11—We should desire God's insight and love.

7. Philippians 2:3-4—We should always be looking out for the other person's best interests.

WRAP-UP

Talk-to (4 minutes)

Summarize what you have discussed and learned about dating in general. (For example, it should be a time to get to know members of the opposite sex; too often we are pressured to play dating "games" or to get involved sexually; dates become too serious, and we can't really get to know the other person; etc.). Challenge group members to date informally and in groups and to be creative about their dates. Then tell them that Christians have a responsibility to *live for Christ* on their dates. This means . . .

- Treating the other person with respect
- Being honest with your feelings
- Not using the other person to meet your own needs
- Being loving toward him or her
- Building friendships with many members of the opposite sex
- Making sure that the date itself is honoring to Christ

Guidelines (4 minutes)

Using the backs of their *Love Lists* papers, have group members jot down specific steps they can take to improve their dating lives. Encourage them to refer to the

biblical principles that you listed earlier and to the points you made in your talk. While they are writing, make specific suggestions like: **Ask someone out to do something fun, relaxing, and inexpensive; plan the next date well in advance so as not to have any leftover "miscellaneous" time at the end; don't put yourself in tempting situations; talk over creative, new dating options with friends; etc.** Encourage them to talk to you about specific problems or questions they might have. Close in prayer.

Make sure that they take this seriously. Offer to hold them accountable for their personal strategy if they wish.

Options for Further Study

Group Date—Give your students the assignment of planning, and going on, a group date. There should be no couples. The date should include as many of the girls/guys in the group as possible. They should do the following:

1. Plan the evening activity: Where? When? Who's paying?
2. Go on the date.
3. Evaluate the date: What did each person enjoy? Why did he or she enjoy it? Did you learn anything new about anyone? What would you do differently next time?

Blind Date—This is a *real* blind date which you chaperone. Choose two young people who do not know each other and arrange an evening for the date. Pick up the boy at his house and blindfold him. Then drive to the girl's house, blindfold her, and lead her to the car where she meets her date. Do the entire date blindfolded. Then at your next meeting, introduce them to each other and have them explain how the date went and how they felt.

Choose these young people carefully, and let them know ahead of time what you will be doing.

Additional Resources

The Stork Is Dead (Charlie Shedd, Word)
A very practical and down to earth discussion of sex.

A Love Story (Tim Stafford, Tyndale House)
Questions and answers on love, sex, dating, and related issues taken from Tim's popular column in *Campus Life* magazine, "Love, Sex, and the Whole Person."

GETTING ALONG WITH BROTHERS AND SISTERS

1 JOHN 2:9–11; 4:19–21
1 TIMOTHY 5:8

SESSION 15

BROTHERS AND SISTERS

HOW CAN I IMPROVE MY RELATIONSHIPS WITH MY BROTHERS AND SISTERS?

KEY CONCEPT	Sibling rivalries and conflicts are a normal part of life for most young people.
GOAL	This session will challenge young people to see the importance of living for Christ at home where often it is most difficult.
OVERVIEW	Though Christians are supposed to love people, and especially their own families, conflicts with brothers and sisters are very common. When you live with someone, he or she knows your weaknesses and faults and knows how to anger or hurt you. And there is the continual, normal, everyday friction caused by being close together. But a person's faith must "work" at home if it is to work anywhere. This inconsistency between what their lives should be and what they are at home can be very frustrating to young people. This session, therefore, will discuss why and how they can live for Christ in their families, especially with their brothers and sisters. During this session, be sure to let your young people know that some conflict is normal and they should work through it together. But also emphasize their responsibility to be people who are living for Christ and acting in love.
TIME REQUIRED	30–45 minutes

MATERIALS CHECKLIST

Materials needed for basic session:
____ Copies of *Brothers Quiz*   ____ Case studies to read
____ Pencils or pens   ____ New Testaments
____ Questions (*Brothers/Sisters Panel*) ____ Cards or pieces of paper (*Changes*)
____ Copies of *Sibling Questionnaire*

Materials needed for optional activities:
____ Candles, matches, glasses, and prize (*Candle Blowing Contest*)
____ Participants and washrag (*The Fly Family*)

JUNIOR HIGH ADAPTATION

For this session to be most effective, begin with *The Fly Family* and then move into the *Sibling Questionnaire*. Follow these activities with *Case Studies* and then go into the *Bible Study*. Finish the session the way it is written, using junior high examples in your *Wrap-up*.

WARM-UP

Optional Openers

Candle Blowing Contest (6–8 minutes)

Ask for two volunteers from the crowd. On a table between them place two candles and a large box of matches. Give each person a glassful of water. The object of the game is to be the first one to drink his glass of water; however, they may only drink water while their candles are lit. The strategy is obvious: each person should try to keep his candle lit so he can drink, but he should blow out the other's so he can't. For best results, have somebody helping to hold the outside striking surfaces of the matchboxes steady so the contestants can continue to strike their matches. Also, the candles must remain stationary on the table. Assign a referee to make sure nobody is drinking water while his candle is not lit. Award a prize to the winner, and repeat with two others if you have time.

Protect the table and floor from water and wax. The object of this activity is to have fun and to illustrate the kinds of conflicts that arise between people, even loved ones.

The Fly Family (4–5 minutes)

Choose someone from the crowd to meet the "Fly Family" (a group of students who are standing in the front with their hands behind their backs). Introduce him or her to the family one at a time. The family members are "Mr. Horse Fly," "Ms. Butterfly," "Mr. Tsetse Fly," and "Ms. House Fly." Each "fly" person shakes hands with him or her. The final family member to be introduced is "Mr. Letter Fly." As soon as he is introduced, instead of shaking hands, he throws a wet washrag in the face of the unsuspecting victim. To do this with more than one "victim," take them out of the room, and bring them in one at a time.

Because this game can be embarrassing to the "victims," choose those who can take a joke. Afterward, commend them on being good sports and build them up in front of the crowd. The object of this game is to have fun and to begin to think about families.

Brothers Quiz (5 minutes)

Hand out copies of the following quiz and instruct group members to fill in the famous brothers described. (Answers are in parentheses.)

The purpose of this activity is to begin to focus on brothers and sisters.

BROTHERS QUIZ

1. TV detectives _____ (Simon and Simon)
2. Old Testament antagonists _____ (Jacob and Esau)
3. '50s singers _____ (Everly Brothers)
4. The first brothers _____ (Cain and Abel)
5. Fictional Russian brothers _____ (Brothers Karamazov)
6. His brothers sold him _____ (Joseph)
7. Former President's infamous, younger brother _____ (Billy Carter)
8. Jesus' disciples _____ (James and John)
9. Funny folk singers _____ (Smothers Brothers)
10. Jesus' earthly brother _____ (James)
11. For extra credit, list other famous brothers. _____

Give the answers and acknowledge the winner.

Sibling Questionnaire (8 minutes)

Hand out the following questionnaire (or hand out paper and read the questions one at a time).

When you reproduce this questionnaire, leave room for answers. Don't get bogged down in the discussion. It is important, but this is a *Warm-up* activity.

SIBLING QUESTIONNAIRE

1. Circle the correct title to the famous song:
   - Ain't He Heavy, Brother?
   - He Ain't Heavy, or My Brother!
   - Heavy Ain't the Word, Brother!
   - He Ain't Heavy, I Am.
   - He Ain't Heavy, You Should See My Older Brother!
   - He Ain't Heavy, She's My Sister!
   - He Ain't My Brother, He's Just heavy!
   - He Ain't Heavy _____ (fill in the blank)
2. Of all the people in the world, who would you most enjoy having as a brother or sister?
3. How many people in this room included you on their lists? Why or why not?
4. Do you know any real families in which brothers and/or sisters get along well? Why?
5. What do you think it would take to improve your relationship with your brother or sister?

Take the answers one at a time and discuss them together skipping question three.

Brothers/Sisters Panel (8 minutes)

Choose three or four "volunteers" from the audience to participate in an "on-the-spot" panel discussion. These panel members should be young people who have brothers and/or sisters. Seat them in front of the group and then ask them these questions.

For their answers to these questions, panel members should think of *one* brother or sister, except for question 5.

1. What does your brother/sister say that bothers you the most?
2. What was the last argument between you and your brother/sister?
3. What was the most memorable experience you shared together?
4. When do you feel the closest to him or her?
5. How are you and your brother(s)/sister(s) alike? Different?
6. When was the last time you came to his/her aid, help, or defense?

WORKOUT

Case Studies (10 minutes)

Read the following case studies and after each one ask: **What do we know about each person in the story?** and **What would you do if you were _____?**

These case studies may not fit your "culture." Make the necessary adaptations or write new ones. The idea is for them to put themselves into the specific situations, to determine what all the characters are like, to identify with the main character, and to choose a course of action.

Case Study #1

Matt is a sophomore in high school and is the oldest child of three in his family: Tim is in seventh grade, and Janet is in fourth. When they were younger, Matt and Tim used to play together, but lately, Tim is getting on Matt's nerves, always bringing his junior high friends over to the house and messing around with Matt's games. They've argued a lot lately. Last Tuesday, Matt came home from basketball practice and went into his room. It was a mess! Someone had been playing with his electronic basketball game and had left it out, *and* his favorite mug lay broken on the floor. He stomped out of his room, looking for Tim.

Case Study #2

Becki is sick of hearing about her older sister Jayne—"Miss Perfect." It seems like all Mom and Dad can say or imply is that she should be like Jayne, the

straight-A student and all-state swimmer. Jayne's a senior and Becki a sopho-more, and the teachers always call Becki by her sister's name and expect them to be alike. Last night at dinner, Becki blew up, screaming at Jayne and saying she hated her and wished she weren't her sister. Then she stomped out, went to her room, and slammed the door. Later Dad came up and said she was grounded. Today, Becki feels bad for what she did, but she feels like a second-class citizen in her own home. Down deep she loves her sister, but the whole situation is frustrating.

Ask for suggestions for other "case studies" and discuss them.

Bible Discussion (5 minutes)

Explain that it probably has been pretty obvious that the topic for this session is getting along with brothers and sisters. Then, give group members the following passages, one at a time, and ask them to look up the verses and to answer the question: **What does this say about how Christians should relate to their brothers and sisters?** Possible answers in parentheses.

1. 1 John 2:9–11 (If you hate your brother, you are not walking in the light—a true Christian.)
2. 1 John 4:19–21 (If you truly love God, you will love your brother.)
3. 1 Timothy 5:8 (The worst kind of person neglects the family.)

These verses come on very strong; don't minimize their message.

Next, discuss how they feel after reading these verses which come on very strong about our responsibility for our brothers and sisters. Discuss the following questions:

1. **When do you feel "hateful" toward family members? Why?**
2. **How do you show love toward your brother(s) and/or sister(s)?**
3. **What causes most of your conflicts with your brother(s) and/or sister(s)?**

Next, have everyone turn to 1 Corinthians 13, the love chapter, and have them find specific verses which may be applied to their home situations. Discuss these briefly.

Make sure their answers are specific (i.e. not "love them," etc.).

WRAP-UP

Talk-to (4 minutes)

Summarize the session with the following points:

1. **As Christians, we are expected to love everyone ... especially our families.**
2. **Conflict is normal when people live together.**
3. **Most conflicts can be resolved by one person taking the "love initiative."**
4. **Biblical, Christian love is commitment and action, not feelings.**
5. **Most of us really love our family members though we don't often feel it or show it.**
6. **Your brothers and sisters are *people*, special creations of God for whom Christ died. They are not "things," "inconveniences," or "annoyances."**
7. **Life is short, and soon we will be separated from those we love.**
8. **Commit to being a loving person *now* in your home; it will revolutionize your relationships.**

Changes (5 minutes)

Give everyone a card or piece of paper and this assignment: **Open to 1 Corinthians 13 again and look especially at verses 4–7. Then write down two changes you will make, with God's help, in your relationship with a brother or sister.** Challenge group members to pray about these changes daily and to make them. Close in prayer.

Option for Further Study

Brainstorm ways to build better relationships with brothers and sisters, especially younger ones. One possibility would be to design a series of questions which would facilitate discussion between them. They could "interview" a brother or sister and report back the next week with their findings.

Additional Resources

The Birth Order Book (Kevin Lehman, Fleming H. Revell)
Dr. Lehman explains how a child's birth order affects his or her personality and temperament. This would give young people helpful insight into why they and their siblings act the way they do.

Traits of a Healthy Family (Dolores Curran, Winston Press)
This is a positive approach to family, outlining the top 15 strengths found in healthy families.